Guid
reco
lear

Guidelines for Colleges: recommendations for learning resources

Edited by
Andrew Eynon
for the Colleges of Further and Higher Education Group of CILIP

Working Party
Kathy Ennis, Carole Gray, Lin Watson

facet publishing

© CILIP: the Chartered Institute of Library and Information Professionals, 1965, 1971, 1982, 1990, 1995, 2000, 2005

Published by
Facet Publishing
7 Ridgmount Street
London WC1E 7AE

Facet Publishing (formerly Library Association Publishing) is wholly owned by CILIP: the Chartered Institute of Library and Information Professionals.

First published 1965
Second edition 1971
Third edition 1982
Fourth edition 1990
Fifth edition 1995
Sixth edition published under the title *Guidelines for Learning Resource Services in Further and Higher Education: performance and resourcing* 2000
This seventh edition 2005

British Library Cataloguing in Publication Data
A catalogue record for this book is available from the British Library.

ISBN 1-85604-551-X

Typeset from editors' disks by Facet Publishing Production in 10.5/14pt Nimbus Roman and Nimbus Sans.
Printed and made in Great Britain by MPG Books Ltd, Bodmin, Cornwall.

Contents

Foreword

It is a great honour to be asked to write the Foreword to the *Guidelines for Colleges: recommendations for learning resources*, produced by CoFHE, one of CILIP's special interest groups. This edition, like others before it, is 'new and improved', incorporating information from a recent survey of FE colleges as well as including new sections relevant to professional practice across the education sector.

My presidential themes are about improving the profession through reflective and evidence-based practice, both of which require access to the knowledge base of the library and information profession. These *Guidelines* provide library and information staff in the HE and FE sectors with this evidence of good practice and professional standards.

As an HE librarian myself, I am aware of the rapidly changing environment in education which brings new challenges – in meeting the needs of an increasingly diverse user population, providing access to a rapidly growing pool of learning resources, and all the time demonstrating value for money. I am delighted that these *Guidelines* are so well contextualized and that the key topics of information literacy, customer care, advocacy and inclusion are highlighted. The new section on benchmarking is also very useful as we all endeavour to demonstrate our contribution to our particular institution's success.

The ten recommendations are straightforward, achievable and entirely consistent with the mission of CILIP, the values of our profession, and the priorities in the DfES 5 Year Strategy. HE and FE colleges which implement these recommendations will be making a significant step forward in supporting the learning of their students and their communities.

I congratulate all those who contributed to the new edition.

Margaret Haines
President, CILIP, 2004-5
Director of Information Services and Systems, King's College London

Acknowledgements

My sincere thanks go to the *Guidelines* working party: Carole Gray (Dundee College), Lin Watson (Exeter College) and Kathy Ennis (CILIP). I would also like to thank members of the CoFHE national committee, and other interested parties who contributed to the revision of the draft version of these *Guidelines*. Finally the working party owes a debt of gratitude to Fiona Murray, Subject Librarian at the College of Food, Tourism and Creative Studies, for her assistance in providing us with a computer during the drafting of these *Guidelines* on a visit to Birmingham in March 2004.

Recommendations

1   Every further education institution should have a learning resource service which exists to meet the information needs of the staff and student communities it serves.
2   Learning resource services have a key role to play in enhancing the life skills of the community they serve through the effective promotion of information skills and information literacy.
3   The learning resource service should develop a mission statement, and aims and objectives, in line with the college's own. These should be determined in consultation with the various client groups who make use of the service.
4   The learning resource service should be part of a robust quality system which reflects the requirements of both the college and the various inspection bodies. The quality systems employed by the service could include self-assessment exercises, service level agreements, quality standards and participation in peer assessment.
5   Learning resource managers need to develop the skills necessary to make them effective advocates for the service.
6   Learning resource centres should cater for a variety of learning styles; they should be adequately furnished and equipped, and should reflect an inclusive ethos.
7   Learning resource services need to be accessible to all students, including those with learning disabilities and difficulties, distance learners and those who may feel socially excluded from further education.
8   Learning resource services should develop broad collections, with material provided in a variety of formats to suit the needs of users with differing abilities.
9   Learning resource services should be managed by a Chartered Member of CILIP. The learning resource manager should hold a management position within the institution. Learning resource staff engaged in managing staff or budgets, or responsible for information skills training, should hold a professional library or information qualification.
10   The learning resource service should be adequately funded to ensure that sufficient levels of staff and resources are maintained.

Introduction

These *Guidelines* have been written to assist learning resource managers of further education and sixth form colleges in planning and developing their learning resource services. The advice offered is aimed primarily at librarians working in the further education sector, but the recommendations and guidance covered are appropriate in principle throughout the education sector.

In order for learning resource services to meet the ever changing requirements of governmental agencies (social inclusion, accessibility for all, lifelong learning and 'empowering the learning community') there is a need for relevant, up-to-date and robust guidelines for such provision.

This new edition of the *Guidelines* incorporates the results of the *UK Survey of Library and Learning Resource Provision in Further Education Colleges 2003* (CILIP, 2003). There are new sections on facilitating learning, promotion and advocacy, and accessibility, to reflect new demands on learning resource provision.

In addition, the *Guidelines* include **key recommendations** and **quantitative performance indicators**. **Key recommendations** are shown as R1, R2, R3, etc. at the beginning of each chapter. **Quantitative performance indicators** are shown as PI1, PI2, PI3, etc. at the end of some chapters.

Glossary

The glossary includes general acronyms as well as those used within the text.

AAT	Association of Accounting Technicians
ALF	average level of funding
ALI	Adult Learning Inspectorate
BECTA	British Educational Communications and Technology Agency
C&G	City and Guilds (of London Institute)
CHEST	Combined Higher Education Software Team
CD-ROM	compact disc-read only memory
CIBSE	Chartered Institute of Building Services Engineers
CILIP	Chartered Institute of Library and Information Professionals
CoFHE	Colleges of Further and Higher Education Group (of CILIP)
CoLRiC	Council for Learning Resources in Colleges
CPD	continuing professional development
CVCP	Committee of Vice-Chancellors and Principals of the Universities of the United Kingdom (renamed Universities UK in 2000)
DDA	Disability Discrimination Act 1995
DEL	Department of Employment and Learning Northern Ireland
DES	Department of Education and Science
DfEE	Department for Education and Employment
EARL	Electronic Access to Resources in Libraries
ELWa	Education and Learning Wales
ETI	Education and Training Inspectorate (of the Department of Education, Northern Ireland)
Estyn	Her Majesty's Inspectorate for Education and Training in Wales
FEDA	Further Education Development Agency
FEFC	Further Education Funding Council
FENC	Further Education National Consortium
FERL	Further Education Resources for Learning
FTE	full-time equivalent

HCLRG	Higher Education Funding Councils' Colleges Learning Resources Group
HEFCE	Higher Education Funding Council England
HEFCW	Higher Education Funding Council Wales
HESA	Higher Education Statistics Agency
HMIe	Her Majesty's Inspectorate (Scotland)
ICT	information and communications technology
IIP	Investors in People
ILT	information and learning technology
IPD	Institute of Personnel and Development
JANET	UK Joint Academic and Research Network
JISC	Joint Information Systems Committee
LAMIT	Multimedia and IT Group of CILIP
LCD	liquid crystal display
LIC	Library and Information Commission
LISU	Library and Information Statistics Unit
LRC	learning resource centre
LRDG	Learning Resources Development Group
LRM	learning resource manager
LRS	learning resource service
MLA	Museums, Libraries and Archives Council
NIACE	National Institute for Adult and Continuing Education
NVQ	National Vocational Qualification
OFSTED	Office for Standards in Education
OHP	overhead projector
OPAC	online public access catalogue
QAA	Quality Assurance Agency
RBL	resource-based learning
RRA	Race Relations (Amendment) Act 2000
RSC	Regional Support Centre (JISC)
SCONUL	Standing Conference of National and University Libraries
SCOP	Standing Conference of Principals
SENDA	Special Educational Needs and Disability Act 2001
SFEFC	Scottish Further Education Funding Council
SLIC	Scottish Library and Information Council
SPUR	Student Powered Unit of Resource (Northern Ireland)
SUM	student unit of measurement (Scotland)
SVQ	Scottish Vocational Qualification
SWOT	strengths, weaknesses, opportunities and threats
TechDis	The JISC service that supports the needs of disabled staff and students in FE and HE through the use of appropriate technology

TQA	Teaching Quality Assessment
TTA	Teacher Training Agency
UC&R	University, College and Research Group (of CILIP)
UCISA	Universities and Colleges Information Systems Association
Ufi	University for Industry
UKOLN	UK Office for Library and Information Networking

1

Facilitating learning

R1
Every further education institution should have a learning resource service which exists to meet the information needs of the staff and student communities it serves.

R2
Learning resource services have a key role to play in enhancing the life skills of the community they serve through the effective promotion of information skills and information literacy.

Why does a college have a learning resource service or library? There is no statutory obligation to provide access to the materials to support and enhance the learning process. Yet this service remains one of the institution's principal educational resources.

The learning resource service exists to support the information needs of all members of the institution: students, teachers, managers and support staff. It provides resources in many formats. It offers the support that users need to plan, locate, retrieve, select, appraise, organize, record and communicate information. It serves the educational process as a learning and information centre, and can support the institution best when closely integrated into the academic process. It is a service that facilitates the interaction between people and the information they need.

The role of the learning resource service is to stimulate and encourage learning; its focus is the learner. The methods by which this is achieved are tangible, for example through teaching information-handling and knowledge-navigation skills, by providing appropriate learning resources or designing physical spaces that encourage independent learning. However, some methods are intangible, such as providing motivation or individual advice, or encouraging communication and interpersonal skills development through the provision of group work spaces.

A learning resource centre is often viewed solely as an extension of the classroom, but it is much more than that. Many learning resource service staff base their case for position and status within an organization on their 'sameness' with their teaching colleagues. They are not the same, they are unique. Learning resource service staff need to raise the profile of the body of skills they posses that makes them different from curriculum staff, the heart of which is the organization of knowledge, the empowerment of the individual by providing access to quality assured information and the promotion of the joy of reading for understanding and pleasure.

In the knowledge society the ability to use information appropriately is only surpassed in importance by the ability to recognize when information is needed. Understanding the nature of a question, recognizing the constituent components of that question, locating the appropriate resources to supply the information necessary to answer the question, filtering out all unnecessary information, reinterpreting the information found and communicating the answer to the question is what a learning resource service is for – it enables a learner to become information literate.

1.1 Information literacy

Information literacy encompasses knowledge of one's information concerns and needs, and the ability to identify, locate, evaluate, organise, and effectively create, use and communicate information to address issues or problems at hand; it is a prerequisite for participating effectively in the Information Society, and is part of the basic human right of lifelong learning
                    The Prague Declaration 'Towards an Information Literate Society',
                    Literacy Meeting of Experts, 20–23 September 2003

The expertise in developing storage and retrieval mechanisms for resources for learning lies with the learning resource service. Therefore it is the responsibility of the learning resource service to ensure that learners are given the opportunity to acquire the skills necessary to operate in an increasingly information- and knowledge-driven society.

The learning resource service provides the support, training and guidance that learners need to locate, retrieve, select, appraise, organize, record, communicate and evaluate information; and it provides an environment in which the skills of information handling can be learned, practised and developed.

Every learning resource service must offer induction and ongoing information-literacy building programmes. These programmes should be integrated, relevant, at the appropriate level and timely.

1.2   Learning styles

What is learning? One definition is:

Learning is a process of active engagement with experience. It is what people do when they want to make sense of the world. It may involve the development or deepening of skills, knowledge, understanding, awareness, values, ideas and feelings, or an increase in the capacity to reflect. Effective learning leads to change, development and the desire to learn more.

MLA definition adapted from the Campaign for Learning Inspiring Learning for All, www.inspiringlearningforall.gov.uk

If this is learning, then how do people learn? The 'how' is usually described as a preferred learning style.

There are many different theories of learning styles: the concept of multiple intelligences; the *VAK Model* of visual, auditory and kinaesthetic learners; the *Herrmann Brain Dominance Instrument*; the Kolb *Learning Styles Inventory*; and Honey and Mumford's *Learning Styles*.

What all these theories have in common is the recognition that different people learn differently. Therefore the learning resource centre must cater for the differing learning styles of students.

An optimal learning environment would provide:

- *a positive environment*: where learners feel relaxed, stimulated, safe, interested and able to socialize
- *opportunities for involvement*: where learners are actively involved, participate in decision making and feel 'ownership' of the environment
- *opportunities for collaboration*: where collaboration, team work, social interaction and a sense of community are encouraged
- *variety*: where learners have access to a variety of learning options and resources, where they are able to use all their senses, and where they are able to practise their preferred learning style
- *a context*: where learners are provided with the resources that put their learning into perspective and they are evaluated, given feedback and the opportunity for reflection.

The size and shape of a learning resource centre may not lend itself easily to creating these varying environments but, at the very least, there should be areas for silent study, quiet study and group work. The development of areas for discussion, social interaction and self-expression should be considered.

In Chapter 4 of these *Guidelines* environmental issues are discussed in far more detail. However, although providing for different learning styles can be problematic, it is the responsibility of the learning resource staff – as experts – to work closely with senior managers to formulate appropriate solutions if the learning resource centre is to be effective learning space.

1.3   Learner support

The provision of circulation control systems (lending books), enquiry services, internet access and catalogues are housekeeping activities that must not be confused with the primary function of the learning resource service. The learning resource centre is a complex mechanism staffed by people whose task is to provide the right piece of information to the right person at the right time.

Learning resource staff play an important learner support role: providing quality controlled information; advising learners on the most appropriate materials to support their learning needs; and guiding them through the maze of resources available within their own collections and a range of national and international resources.

However, because learning resource centres are viewed by learners as a neutral, non-threatening environment, learning resource staff often find themselves fulfilling a role similar to that of their teaching colleagues, and other support staff in, for example, student counselling and guidance services.

Therefore it is essential for all learning resources staff to have access to customer care, basic skills, advice and guidance, and other appropriate training.

1.4   Reader development

Reader development is the development of the individual through reading. It is reader-centred, in that the reading experience – not the author, or the subject, or the theme of the book – is as important as the enjoyment of what is being read.

The impetus for reader development activity stems from the public library sector. The term 'reader development' is now commonly used in government reports as it has been shown to have a significant impact on agendas such as social inclusion, literacy and citizenship.

In further education and sixth form colleges reading for pleasure among students is practically non-existent. This is not helped by the fact that in many cases budgets will not stretch to financing interesting and vibrant collections of fiction materials.

There is also the question of the relevance of reader development in post-16 education. Small-scale projects in further education colleges have shown that reader development is relevant as it can be used to enhance the curriculum. Examples include:

• teaching nursery nursing students to choose appropriate story books and story-telling techniques

- forensic science students comparing their work to that of Kay Scarpetta (Patricia Cornwell)
- using Verne's *Around the World in 80 Days* with travel and tourism students to compare attitudes to travel.

In further education reader development is a unique skill that learning resources staff can bring to the development of the learner.

1.5   Sectoral and cross-sectoral collaboration

In terms of the provision of library and learning resource services further education is not unique. The agendas that drive the post-16 learning sector are the same agendas that are influencing the public, private and corporate sectors. The questions, issues and dilemmas that arise daily in further education are exactly the same questions, issues and dilemmas that affect colleagues in other sectors – they just use different jargon.

Many learning resource managers and their staff take time and effort to develop processes, practices and procedures for their workplace that somebody else has already developed elsewhere.

Sectoral and cross-sectoral collaboration is essential as it will provide fresh eyes, new ideas, a different perspective, and opportunities for personal and professional development.

2

A quality framework

R3
The learning resource service should develop a mission statement, and aims and objectives, in line with the college's own. These should be determined in consultation with the various client groups who make use of the service.

R4
The learning resource service should be part of a robust quality system which reflects the requirements of both the college and the various inspection bodies. The quality systems employed by the service could include self-assessment exercises, service level agreements, quality standards and participation in peer assessment.

Quality is hard to define but everyone feels they recognize it. To measure the quality of a service or demonstrate it in quantitative terms is notoriously difficult. The standard definition of quality, which is often cited, is that of 'fitness for purpose'.

To enable the fitness for purpose of a learning resource service to be assessed a number of factors must be present. They are:

- a quality policy
- a statement of mission and aims of the learning resource service which stem from the mission and aims of the institution
- a process of review and systematic strategic and operational planning
- a means of measuring needs and satisfaction levels of users
- a means of relating learning resources policies to the needs and wishes of users
- a review mechanism based on internal evaluation and external inspection or assessment.

2.1   Quality policy

A quality policy document is the record of the systems and procedures which are in place to ensure that users have a satisfactory experience and that quality continues to improve. Many institutions have introduced service level agreements (SLAs) to cover all or part of their provision.

A quality policy must:

- specify the aims and objectives of the service
- specify the procedures for monitoring the delivery of those aims and objectives
- include a manual or documentation of procedures, for example a set of quality standards and how they are reviewed
- include mechanisms for collecting data to evaluate effectiveness
- include a feedback loop to ensure that identified weaknesses are dealt with
- indicate a culture which stresses that quality is the responsibility of all staff.

Many quality systems exist such as ISO 9000, Total Quality Management (TQM), Investors in People (IIP), target setting and peer assessment or accreditation. Public libraries have been using the Best Value Review (BVR) model and many of the findings of the Audit Commission's *Building Better Library Services* [1] apply equally to academic libraries.

Under the BVR model LRS are asked to answer the following key questions regarding their provision:

- Do we meet the needs of our learners/customers?
- Do we provide value for money?
- How does our service compare?
- Do we have an effective review process?
- Are we delivering the improvements?

Learning resource managers must decide which method best suits the needs of their own institution. Whatever system is used will need to match that used by the parent institution and meet the requirements of any inspecting, awarding or validating bodies.

2.2   Mission statement

Like any business the learning resource service needs a clearly defined mission in order to focus its work and to assist forward planning.

Mission statements vary but they should all describe the learning resource service's basic purpose, derived from the parent institution's mission statement, and relate to the institution's organizational structure.

A typical statement might be:

To provide an innovative, responsive and proactive learning resource service supporting the learning, teaching, and research needs of the user community, in such a way as to meet its requirements and expectations and achieve the highest professional standards in a cost effective, stimulating and user friendly manner.

The formulation of a mission statement is a group activity. Therefore the learning resource service mission statement should be developed with the co-operation of all learning resource service staff and reflect the needs of the service's users.

2.3   Aims

The aims of the learning resource service should be formulated in a process of consultation between the service's staff, its users, the academic board and senior management. The aims should reflect the mission statements of the institution *and* the learning resource service.

A typical statement of aims might be:

- To identify and provide access to the learning resource services required to support the learning, teaching and research activities of the institution
- To manage those resources efficiently, effectively and economically
- To establish an environment conducive to study and which caters for multiple learning styles and for individual and group learning
- To liaise with boards of study or course committees and students to establish their requirements and to co-operate with management and other support services to meet these needs
- To teach users about the learning resource service facilities and to develop their information skills
- To maintain effective links with staff of the institution in order to understand and, where necessary, respond to changes in education, approaches to learning, and corporate policy
- To ensure learning resource provision and facilities are accessible to all
- To ensure learning resources staff have the appropriate technical skills, qualifications and experience
- To ensure that the service offered is to the highest quality and is subject to the principles of continuous improvement.

Aims cannot be static. They should be regularly reviewed and amended in the light of alterations in the mission statements and by referral to the relevant performance standards.

It is essential that when institutional policy documents are being drafted or revised, their impact on the learning resource service should be considered, and resource implications taken into account. Such institutional documents might include policy statements, strategic or marketing plans, student charters and contracts, codes of conduct, and grievance and disciplinary procedures.

2.4   Objectives

Objectives are more specific than aims. They are the outcomes that satisfy the aims, and they must be measurable and achievable within resource and time constraints.

For example, if the aim is:

to establish an environment conducive to study and which caters for multiple learning styles and for individual and group learning

then the objectives might include:

- the identification of the balance between individual and group study requirements
- the provision of appropriate ICT or ILT
- the staffing requirements.

Objectives should be set in such terms that it is possible to measure their fulfilment against service standards, performance measures, indicators and benchmarks.

2.5   Strategic and operational planning

Planning is an integrated process of making decisions by bringing together a series of ideas so that they can relate to each other and form a rational whole to establish the action to be taken.

The strategic plan of a learning resource service will be drawn up as part of the planning cycle of the institution. In simple terms strategic management can be described as:

a plan of action to enable an organisation to move from where it is now to where it wants to be at a future date. Managers need to have an idea about where they want the organisation to be in the future and the route it is going to follow to get there.[2]

Strategic management is not just about planning it also about consistency of approach and about evaluating past behaviour as well as being responsive to changing external factors.

Sheila Corrall (2000) has summarized the main purposes of strategic management in a library context as being:

- to clarify purpose and objectives
- to determine directions and priorities
- to encourage a broader-based longer-term view
- to identify critical issues and constraints
- to provide a framework for policy and decisions
- to inform resource allocation and utilization.[3]

The operational plan is a time-dependent subset of the strategic plan, constructed from the identified objectives and targets. In most instances a strategic plan highlights the key priorities of the institution or service. The operational plan focuses more on how these key objectives will be met.

However, before operational planning can begin, an evaluation of the existing service, and an analysis of how it fits with other services in the institution, needs to be undertaken in order to determine where improvements can or need to be made. This is usually in the form of a self-assessment exercise, which is usually conducted in a format prescribed by the organization. The Scottish Further Education Funding Council has produced *Resources and Services Supporting Learning: a service development quality toolkit*.[4] It is a self-assessment quality framework specifically for further education colleges, which covers the following graded elements (with examples):

- learning resource organization
- staffing
- ICT integration
- user support
- accessibility
- inclusiveness
- quality assurance and improvement.

Both the strategic and operational plans of the learning resource service relate directly to the parent institution's development or strategic plan, and are informed by the learning resource service's mission, aims, objectives and targets as reflected in the service's own self-assessment exercise.

Aspects of learning resource provision could be evaluated in the following terms:

- State the objective (or relevant professional standard) you are evaluating the service against, for example, that the service is adequately staffed. These

objectives (or quality standards) could be drawn from the relevant external inspection framework for the institution.
- What is the performance indicator or target for this objective, for example, the ratio of staff to students?
- What is the current position of the service?
- Is this a strength or weakness?
- What is the evidence used to substantiate this position statement?

The self-assessment exercise or review of the service's aims and objectives will highlight those areas which need to be addressed in strategic or operational plans. From this process targets, which are the most specific part of the strategic management process, will be set. They form what is often called the 'action plan'. Targets are essential for the control of tasks, and the achievement of objectives.

Action plans include the following elements:

- the objective that is going to be addressed; this could be a weakness identified in the self-assessment exercise or it could be a new area of provision for the service
- the action point – what needs to be done, including any applicable quantitative targets
- the identification of who is going to meet these targets
- the identification of any additional resources that will be required
- a target completion date
- a review date, to see if the target has been, or is likely to be, met.

2.6   Performance measurement

Performance measures are used to gauge how well a service fulfils its purpose. Despite much debate about performance indicators there remains no universally accepted set of measures; however, there are a number of widely accepted standards that can be used to evaluate learning resource services in academic institutions including CoLRiC criteria for peer accreditation, CoLRiC performance impact indicators (PIIs), SCONUL performance indicators, SLIC/SLA *Standards for Performance and Resourcing* (1997) and the CoFHE *Guidelines*.

Deciding what to measure is difficult but should always be related to the aims and objectives of the parent organization and thence to the purpose of the service being measured, as well as to the requirements of external inspection agencies. In deciding what to measure it is vital to consider the purpose of the measurements being collected. They can be used to aid the effective management of the learning resource service and to demonstrate the contribution of the service to the institution as a whole.

Performance indicators cannot remain static. They will need to change over time and will themselves need continual evaluation in order to ensure their relevance to current issues within the learning resource service, the institution of which it forms a part and the wider educational sphere. Refer to the performance indicators in section **2.11**.

Measurements can be split into two main types:

- quantitative data, such as annual issues or expenditure per full-time equivalent (FTE) and
- qualitative data, such as self-assessment reports, feedback forms and focus groups (refer to the checklist **2.12**)

Management data form the basis from which performance measures can be derived, and as such should be as efficient, consistent and as reliable as possible. The library management system should be used to produce this management data. This data, which should be an integral function of performance measurement, is an essential management tool that aids planning and helps justify the service. It is not merely a tool for operational management but a stimulus to strategic planning.

2.7   Benchmarking and comparative data

Benchmarking provides useful sources of evidence for evaluating learning resource services.

Benchmarking is often described as a method of comparing like with like. It has two elements:

- the comparison of key data obtained from similar institutions
- the comparison of systems, that is, how things are done, within similar institutions.

It is thus particularly useful in assessing performance, as there is a danger, when comparing figures alone, of not taking into account the different approaches and parameters within which each service operates.

Comparative data sources tend to be numerically based. Examples include:

- *UK Survey of Library and Learning Resource Provision in Further Education Colleges 2003*[5] (the survey results are broken down by region, enabling you to identify benchmarks by geographical area)
- the SCONUL annual learning resource service statistics
- UK higher education library management statistics (SCONUL).

2.8   User satisfaction

In evaluating any learning resource service, it is vital to ensure that users of all types remain the focal point of any evaluation. Users of academic learning resource services are not a homogeneous group; they include students, distance learners, teaching and support staff, researchers and external users.

For most learning resource services customer satisfaction is the primary driver of quality and is well described by Peter Brophy's 'Seven key concepts of quality management':

- being clear who the customer is
- listening to the customer
- defining the service clearly
- delivering the service consistently
- monitoring service delivery
- continuous improvement
- delighting the customer.[6]

Students are not a single group; different types of students have different needs. They depend on factors such as academic level, mode of attendance, location, age, disability, language, and methods of teaching and learning. There is no 'typical student' and therefore no easily agreed description of what a student needs from a learning resource service.

Staff, too, have varying needs and requirements. The needs of the managers of an institution will be very different from those of teaching and support staff.

External users can include local business people, distance learners, school children, members of the general public, learndirect and Open University students and students from other colleges or institutions.

Any system of quality measurement must consider all users and try to meet their needs wherever possible. It is also vital to consider non-users and to try to ascertain why potential users do not use the service.

Many issues can influence user satisfaction levels, some of which are identified below:

1 *Resources*
   - The number, range and format of the learning resources should be sufficient to meet the learning, teaching and research needs of students and staff.
   - The learning resources should be well organized and maintained in strict order.
   - The building, facilities and materials should be appropriate for their purpose.

2 *Atmosphere and ambience*
- The service should be open at times convenient to most users.
- The atmosphere should be welcoming and friendly.
- All areas should be clean and tidy.
- The facilities should be visible, easy to use and clearly signed.
- There should be a comfortable working environment where users feel personally secure.
- The service should cater for a variety of learning styles, which should be reflected in the provision of different types of study area with appropriate restrictions on noise levels.

3 *Service credibility and reliability*
- The service should be seen to contain current information and have appropriate older material available.
- The staff should provide appropriate help and advice.
- The service should be reliable, dependable and efficient.

4 *Staff*
- The staff should be polite, attentive and friendly.
- The staff should be able to communicate effectively.
- The staff should be able to gauge the needs of users.

This list does not attempt to be comprehensive but indicates some of the factors that influence user satisfaction levels.

The means of gathering information include surveys, questionnaires, feedback forms, focus groups, user groups and committees, and comments and suggestions from individuals, course teams, committees or other forms of institutional evaluation.

The information gathered could then be used to form the basis of a service charter, a set of service standards or a service level agreement.

2.9   Internal inspection and peer assessment

A crucial element of the quality approach is the ability to demonstrate the provision of a quality service. This can be carried out by a mixture of inspection, evaluation and assessment.

All organizations need to have internal inspection or validation procedures in addition to such external procedures as may exist. Procedures such as SWOT analysis, action planning, target setting and performance measurement as detailed above can be used.

However, it is often difficult for those directly responsible for a service to stand back and evaluate provision objectively. Learning resource managers may wish to invite other people, either from within their own institution, or fellow professionals from other institutions, to carry out evaluations.

Learning resource services in further education and sixth form colleges may choose to use the CoLRiC Peer Accreditation Scheme, which uses trained assessors, to assess learning resource services and award a grade to that service. The Scheme uses a five-tier rating system based on the ability to fulfil a number of criteria, which are either mandatory, core or supportive. A certificate is awarded to services that achieve excellence.

Other local schemes exist. In the Merseyside region, for example, the Circle of Merseyside College Librarians also has a peer evaluation scheme available for the learning resource services of further education and sixth form colleges in Lancashire, Merseyside, Cheshire and North Wales.

Whatever method is used, self-assessment will generally form an essential part of any formal inspection or validation process.

2.10 External inspection and assessment

Inspections of learning resources in further and higher education are carried out by a number of bodies, for example:

- OFSTED, HEFCE, Estyn (Wales), DEL (Northern Ireland), QAA, Her Majesty's Inspectorate of Education (Scotland) and ALI
- franchising bodies
- awarding and validating bodies
- IIP awarding bodies.

During inspections learning resource services will find that they are assessed as part of the inspections of individual subject areas and of cross-college services and facilities.

Guidelines exist for higher and further education inspections. SCONUL has produced *The Quality Assurance Agency for Higher Education - Aide-Mémoire for Reviewers Evaluating Learning Resources*,[7] which acts as an adjunct to QAA's *Handbook for Academic Review*.

OFSTED in England has guidance notes for inspectors contained within its *Handbook for Inspecting Colleges*; while in Wales Estyn inspectors have an *Aide Mémoire - Learning Resources*. In Scotland HMIe quality indicators are listed in *Standards and Quality in Scottish Further Framework for Scottish FE Colleges* (2004).[8] The Council for Learning Resources in Colleges has produced *CoLRiC Guidelines for Self-assessment of College Learning Resource Services*.[9]

Inspections, validations and accreditation visits usually seek to evaluate the quality of the learning resource provision by finding evidence and information about the following:

1 Management and planning – these areas will be investigated:
   - the remit of the learning resource service within the institution's strategic plan and mission statement
   - whether the learning resource service has its own mission statement and aims and objectives
   - the position of the learning resource service within the institution's structure
   - the perceived professional identity and responsibilities of the learning resource staff
   - the procedures for establishing the learning resource budget
   - whether SLAs are in place with departments and/or other user groups.

2 Organizational structure – these areas will be investigated:
   - how the learning resource service is organized, including the grading of staff
   - systems for liaising with other departments within the institution
   - integration of learning resources into curriculum delivery
   - the existence of separate departmental collections, which are not accessible to all students.

3 Learning resource provision – these areas will be investigated:
   - the types of services and facilities provided
   - the level of service provision for stock, equipment, study space, electronic resources, and so on
   - comparison against agreed benchmarks
   - that the needs of all types of users are met, irrespective of race, gender, learning difficulties or disabilities
   - opening hours of the service
   - provision for distance learners
   - provision to work-based learners and those studying at satellite sites
   - the provision of user education support/materials
   - staffing levels.

4 Quality assurance – these areas will be investigated:
   - the systems that exist to collect relevant information on performance
   - evidence that weaknesses are recognized and dealt with; feedback from users and potential users
   - evidence from users and potential users of the service as to how well the service satisfies their needs.

There has been much concern about the way inspections are carried out, particularly in further education, where learning resource services are still not graded separately. A particular concern is that inspectors have little or no experience or expertise in learning resource provision and do not understand or value the contribution of learning resources.

It is the responsibility of learning resource managers and staff in all types of institution to do all they can by the use of detailed self-assessment, peer appraisal and internal inspection to rectify this situation.

At national level it is the responsibility of bodies and groups such CoFHE, UC&R, CoLRiC, SLIC and SCONUL to make the case for quality assurance and inspection systems which recognize the centrality of learning and information resources to quality in learning, teaching and research. These bodies also have a role to play in contributing to the development of such systems.

The case is pursued by contact with quality assurance and inspection bodies, planning and funding agencies, central government and other national sector bodies.

The continued development of resource-based learning, ICT or ILT mediated learning, distance and independent learning add force to the case for adequate quality assurance arrangements for learning resource provision.

2.11 Performance indicators

The following performance indicators (PIs) are derived from the average (median) figures given in CILIP's *UK Survey of Library and Learning Resource Provision in Further Education Colleges 2003*. These PIs should be regarded as a minimum standard. In contrast to previous editions of the *Guidelines* ratios are now to actual student numbers as opposed to FTE figures as it is actual bodies rather than composite ones that make use of learning resources. Figures apply to all institutions, irrespective of size, except where noted.

Physical

Floor space : students	$1m^2$: 10 students
Study space : students	1 : 90 students

Resources

Books : students	3 : 1
Audiovisual materials : students	1 : 10
Periodical subscriptions : students	1 : 100
LRS budget (bookfund) : students	
(excluding staffing costs)	£5 per student

ICT

Open-access PCs : students	1 : 100 (all computers should be internet ready)

Human resources

FTE learning resource staff : students	
(excluding ICT support staff)	1 : 1000

FTE professional staff : students   1 : 5000

There should be a similar ratio (1 : 5000 students) for designated ICT support staff (in addition to the figures above for LRS staff).

Accessibility
Opening hours – a minimum of 50 hours per week in term-time.

2.12 Management data checklist
Quantitative data (efficiency)

This checklist is an updated version of the one prepared by Roddie Shepherd for the 6th edition of the *Guidelines*:

Resources (inputs)

It is sometimes useful to calculate these figures for registered users only.

The physical ratios are:

- floor area : student
- study places : student
- books : student
- audiovisual materials : student
- periodical subscriptions : student
- expenditure on online resource subscriptions : student.

The ICT and ILT ratio is:

- student access terminals : student.

Human ratios are:

- FTE learning resource staff : student
- FTE professional learning resource staff : student
- FTE ICT support staff : student
- FTE learning resource staff : FTE teaching staff.

Financial ratios are:

- total service budget : student
- total service budget as a percentage of total college budget
- staff budget : student

- staff budget as a percentage of total service budget
- staff development budget : member of staff
- staff development budget as a percentage of total service budget
- learning materials budget (bookfund) : student
- learning materials and services budget (bookfund) as a percentage of total service budget
- capital allocation : student.

Time (accessibility) ratios are:

- opening hours: term : FTE learning resource staff
- opening hours: vacation : FTE learning resource staff.

Processes (throughputs)

User education ratios are:

- number of hours : student
- percentage of eligible students attending at least one session
- percentage of students who receive an LRC induction.

The income ratio is:

- total income generated per annum as a percentage of revenue budget.

Learning resources maintenance ratios are:

- items added : student
- items added as a percentage of stock base
- items withdrawn as a percentage of stock base.

The learning resources supply ratio is:

- average time taken to make resources available for loan.

The learning resources losses ratio is:

- value of items lost from stock per annum as a percentage of bookfund.

The interlibrary loans ratio is:

- number of requests for material not satisfied from own stock.

Use of services (outputs)

Market penetration outputs are the percentage of eligible:

- students registered with the learning resource service
- staff registered with the learning resource service
- students who are active users of the learning resource service
- staff who are active users of the learning resource service.

Use of time outputs are:

- average occupancy : hours of opening
- median occupancy : hours of opening.

The use of space outputs are:

- occupancy of study spaces at specific times as a percentage of total study places.

Use of learning resources outputs are:

- annual issues : total lending stock
- number of titles borrowed as a percentage of stock
- annual issues : student
- intensity of use of stock by subject area (average number of times an item is borrowed per annum)
- usage of periodical titles.

The enquiries output is:

- number of substantial enquiries (over 5 minutes) : student.

The use of workstations output is:

- use of computers at specific times as a percentage of total number of computer workstations.

Non-routine data collection outputs are:

- percentage of new items borrowed (accessed within a year of purchase)
- items consulted but not borrowed
- percentage of total stock borrowed or consulted per annum
- age profile of learning resource material.

Cost outputs are:
- unit cost of the service (revenue cost per enrolled student)
- unit cost : opening hours.

External indicators are factors outside the control of the LRS. This data can be acquired from your institution or bodies such as LISU, SCONUL and so on. The outputs are:

- average price category of material
- learning resources price inflation by category of material
- college student numbers
- college funding units
- total college budget.

Qualitative data (effectiveness)

Points to consider include:

- consultations with users, for example through focus groups, forums or surveys
- college student perception surveys: large-scale, questionnaire, mainly closed questions, representative sample
- LRS surveys of staff or students
- special group surveys, for example, part-time students, evening students
- special purpose surveys, for example, about success of visit or opening hours
- user education session evaluation forms
- suggestions books, boxes or boards
- complaints procedures
- LRS staff attendance at faculty board, course team or campus council meetings
- inspectors' and assessors' reports
- peer review
- LRS staff appraisal
- LRS staff survey
- learning resource staff – qualifications
- learning resource staff – training undertaken in last 12 months
- customer satisfaction ratings, for instance for opening hours, resource provision, and approachability and helpfulness of staff
- the extent to which users rely on library staff support to complete their studies
- the professional involvement of learning resource staff
- the range and variety of services on offer
- LRS provision at outlying sites
- the provision of web OPACs

- video and DVD viewing facilities
- the provision of group study areas, quiet study areas, teaching areas
- the range of ICT services and equipment on offer, such as scanners and colour printers.

References

1   Audit Commission, *Building Better Library Services*, Audit Commission, 2002.

2   Hannagan, T., *Management: concepts and practices*, Financial Times Management, 1998.

3   Corrall, S., *Strategic Management of Information Services: a planning handbook*, Aslib/IMI, 2000.

4   Scottish Further Education Funding Council, *Resources and Services Supporting Learning: a service development quality toolkit*, SEFC, 2003.

5   Chartered Institute of Library and Information Professionals, *UK Survey of Library and Learning Resource Provision in Further Education Colleges 2003*, CILIP, 2003.

6   Brophy, P., cited in Winkworth, I., Quality Issues and Performance Indicators in Academic Libraries. In Spiller, D. (ed.), *Academic Library Surveys and Statistics in Practice*, LISU, 1998.

7   Society of College, National and University Libraries, *The Quality Assurance Agency for Higher Education - Aide-mémoire for Reviewers Evaluating Learning Resources*, SCONUL, 2003.

8   This can be downloaded at www.hmie.gov.uk.

9   Council for Learning Resources in Colleges, *CoLRiC Guidelines for Self-assessment of College Learning Resource Services*, CoLRiC, 2002.

3

Promotion and advocacy

R5
Learning resource managers need to develop the skills necessary to make them effective advocates for the service.

3.1 Promotion

Promotion is an element of marketing. Where marketing involves a wide range of activities that make sure that you continue to meet the needs of your 'customers' and they get value in return, promotion is the process of keeping the 'product' in the minds of the 'customers'. Promotion helps stimulate demand for the 'product' and involves ongoing advertising and publicity.

Learning resource managers must ensure that the college community can identify and articulate the value of each of the services available from the learning resource service.

Examples of simple promotional activities include:

- an entry in the prospectus, on the website and the intranet
- leaflets and guides to specific services
- information about specifically targeted services in course leaflets and booklets
- induction sessions
- making the information available in alternative formats such as large print, audio and languages other then English.

These methods will assist the learning resources staff to develop awareness of, interest in, desire for and conviction about the value of learning resource services.

All the promotional activity that a learning resource service undertakes must be based firmly on the image the service wants to portray. Therefore it is necessary for the learning resource service staff to determine the image they want to depict as it is essential that what is said in the promotional material matches the experience of the service. For example, posters, leaflets and brochures may describe a learning resource centre that is welcoming and friendly, but if the first thing a new 'customer' sees are signs listing all the things they are not allowed to do, then a welcoming and friendly environment is not what they will have experienced.

Developing a PR plan is one way a learning resource service can manage promotion. If the PR plan is allied to institutional and departmental business and action plans it stands more chance of being successful.

When developing a PR plan there are four key questions that need to be answered:

- *What are the current perceptions of learning resource services?* The answers to this question can be found through, for example, consultation, communication, seeking feedback or using professional support networks as 'critical friends'.
- *Who do you want to target and whose opinion do you want to change?* This will involve identifying specific individuals and groups (do not try and change the whole world at once), speaking to them in their language, relating your promotional material to their concerns and, very importantly, establishing a budget – however small.
- *How do you get there?* There are many ways, including developing a series of ongoing events, offering the learning resource centre for non-learning resource service activities, encouraging learning resource staff to become involved in all college activities, whether directly related or not, ensuring that learning resource staff never join a committee or group without taking on a role, making sure that all learning resource staff are involved in wider professional activities that can bring credibility to the service and the college.
- *Are perceptions changing?* Methods of monitoring and evaluating the promotional activities and their effect must be developed at an early stage; lessons learned can be used to inform future activities. And, essentially, ensure that all successes and impacts are advertised.

More ideas and downloadable resources are available on the American Media and Library PR website at www.ssdesign.com/librarypr/toolbox.html.

3.2   Advocacy

Advocacy is about speaking out and winning influence. Learning resource managers frequently illustrate the importance of their work by describing the delivery of their services. In advocacy terms it is essential that they begin to convey their value in terms of institutional aims and objectives.

There is a strong correlation between the status of the learning resource service and the extent to which it empowers learners. Status determines whether the learning resource service can work collaboratively with teaching departments; it determines whether the learning resource manager operates at a strategic level; it motivates and stimulates; and it clearly demonstrates the extent to which the provision of learning resources is a priority for the college.

The status of the LRS is defined by the organizational structure within which it operates. This structure may inhibit collaboration, demoralize and marginalize the LRS and limit its potential to impact on achievement.

It is essential that a close working relationship is developed between the learning resource manager and the senior management team. This needs to work practically – so that there is a real recognition of the role of the learning resource service in achieving the aims and objectives of the institution and the development of independent learners. The support of senior management is vital if the learning resource manager is to attend all relevant meetings.

Regular meetings with senior management are essential to gain an understanding of college priorities. These meetings are also an opportunity to raise issues of the learning resource service's status such as:

- recognition of the positive impact the learning resource service has on teaching and learning
- the contribution the learning resource service makes to retention and achievement
- the added value learners and the institution gain from the learning resource service
- the areas where support and development would be helpful
- consideration of the developmental needs and training requirements of learning resource service staff
- defining where you want the learning resource service to be within the current organizational structure, in terms of its ability to support teaching and learning
- repercussions for learning resource service staff of organizational change
- how a new structure could help the learning resource service assist the college deliver aspects of provision they wish to develop.

Develop key partnerships. Discuss your plans with relevant senior managers, explaining what you hope to achieve and seek their support.

The learning resource service must deliver within the framework of the college's aims and objectives. The college must deliver local and national educational targets. With the increased devolution of power from Westminster to the national assemblies, the UK's educational agenda has become more and more nation specific. It is therefore crucial to express your relevance in terms of these strategies and know where your learning resource service fits within them.

Frequently these strategies are generic, and learning resource provision will not be specifically mentioned. It is the role of the learning resource service staff to determine how they can help deliver the developments, improvements and changes that are envisaged within their institution. It is increasingly necessary for learning resource managers to be strategic thinkers.

The learning resource service should identify relevant national and local initiatives, mapping current practice against these initiatives and highlighting this to senior managers. The vocabulary of these initiatives should be used in any relevant paperwork and meetings.

Do not be afraid to discontinue current activities in favour of more relevant activities that will deliver important priorities.

A significant barrier that can seriously affect the learning resource service realizing its potential within the college is the gap created between learning resource service staff and teachers through the use of different professional vocabularies.

Therefore, in order to gain recognition, learning resource service staff must assert their value in terms of their impact on learning, improving achievement levels, meeting the needs of learners with differing learning abilities, increasing skill levels and employability and adding value to the learning experience rather than simply describing the levels of service activity.

Advocacy requires a clear identification of:

- the *target audience* that you wish to influence
- the *message* which you want to get across
- the *strategy* which will enable you to get to your audience
- the *evidence* that will influence the audience
- a method of *recording* and *evaluating* progress.

A comprehensive advocacy resource is the American Library Association's online *Library Advocates Handbook*,[1] which includes guidance on building an advocacy framework, developing an action plan for promoting the service and communicating with stakeholders, and the American Library Association's online advocacy resource hub.

Reference

1   www.ala.org/ala/advocacybucket/libraryadvocateshandbook.pdf.

4

The learning environment

The aim of LRS staff should be to create a welcoming learning environment, available and accessible to all the institution's staff and students, well-organized for information provision and conducive to a variety of patterns of learning activities such as quiet study, collaborative group work, one to one tuition or help, group teaching sessions, ICT and ILT mediated learning or learning workshops.

Regulations and recommendations from government departments and funding bodies about various aspects of the learning resource environment should be adhered to and regular assessment of these aspects of provision should take place. In particular, requirements under Part IV of the Disability Discrimination Act 1995 must be complied with.

This chapter will point out design features and factors to consider, contributing to a good learning environment. The key question to ask is: how can we create an environment where students are keen to enter and want to stay to learn?

4.1 Range of accommodation

The accommodation for LRCs will be located in a variety of different physical settings within colleges depending on the institutional learning contexts and the historical decisions about locations.

Many scenarios exist: a single large LRC on several floors of a building; one or more large open access centres with library and ICT and ILT facilities; several smaller resource centres, in some cases attached to subject departments; or a traditional library, more or less separated from other types of learning or ICT and ILT workshops.

An institution may have many sites, near or far, centrally or locally managed. Each may have its own LRC with differing functions and patterns of management. Learning resources may be a converged service within an institution but not necessarily combined physically in the same centre.

4.2   Allocation of space

To a large extent, the size and shape of the accommodation will be pre-determined by the college situation and frequently out of the control of LRMs. If managers are fortunate enough to be able to specify the size and shape of a new build LRC, then it would be helpful to look at the recommendations for public library design in *Better Public Libraries* (2003),[1] which has information about Design Quality Indicators (p.26), and to look at the SCONUL and MLA databases of new buildings for possible places to visit. *Libraries Must Also Be Buildings?* (2002)[2] also has good advice on getting the brief right for any new library building project.

In *Guidance on Floorspace Management in Further Education Colleges*[3] the FEFC recommended that the total area for further education college LRCs should comprise at least 10% of total college area or at least 20% of the total teaching space.

The 2003 CILIP further education survey[4] gives data from the 50% of colleges that responded to the question about the size of the LRC. The following figures indicating existing provision refer to the size of the main library at each college not the total area of LRC space. Unfortunately there is such a wide variation in the results that no conclusive recommendations can be made from the survey about the floor area of college libraries.

In colleges with one LRC, the floor area ranged from 390 m^2 to 729 m^2. Where colleges had more than one LRC, the floor area ranged from 437 m^2 to 1959 m^2. In medium sized colleges, those with between 10,000 up to 18,000 students, the main LRCs had a floor area of approximately 1200 m^2.

These guidelines recommend that the total area of the LRC equates to 1 m^2 to 10 students for all colleges (This figure is based on the median areas for the college).

In addition to spatial requirements, other factors need to be taken into account:

- Convergence – as more functions are incorporated into the LRC the amount of space per student will need to be increased.
- E-Learning and audiovisual learning make a greater demand on space than paper-based learning.
- Economies of scale – one major LRC is more economical than several smaller LRCs but may disadvantage some students because they have to travel to access LRC services.
- Flexible or resource based learning methods – an increased emphasis on these teaching methods is likely to increase the amount of time students spend in LRCs and therefore puts more pressure on space.
- The increasing amount of group study work – this is a curriculum requirement for which LRCs need to make provision.
- Part-time students – a higher proportion of part-time students increases space needs; FTE student numbers do not indicate the number of bodies in a room!
- Students or staff with physical disabilities must have equality of access, which requires more space for circulation.

4.3 Spatial requirements within learning resource centres

The essential physical feature of a LRC is that the layout is sufficiently accessible for student and staff information needs.

Wherever learning materials and information services are provided there should be adequate space for:

- all types of users to circulate freely, particularly at entrances and exits
- users to find and retrieve both paper-based and electronic learning materials and information
- individuals and small groups of users to work and study quietly
- collaborative group work
- LRS staff to assist and teach individuals and groups
- LRS staff to operate issue and enquiry desks
- LRS staff to have their own work space
- suitable storage of all types of learning materials.

The SCONUL briefing paper *Space Requirements for Academic Libraries and Learning Resource Centres* (1996)[5] makes three practical suggestions to combat problems associated with space, recommending a flexible, but focused, space management:

- Convert storage space to seating space by using high density storage systems.
- Use radical stock disposal policies to create more space.
- Extend opening hours to allow students greater access.

Switching from print materials to electronic resources can save a lot of space!

4.4 Design and layout in learning resource centres

A number of design principles were highlighted in previous CoFHE publications *Library Design* (1992)[6] and *Designs on Learning* (1996).[7] These are good starting points when considering the interior design of LRCs:

- Design from the inside out – think about the activities that need to take place in a LRC before the need for it to fit into a certain shape.
- Design for purpose – how many users? which services? what type of learning materials?
- Design for specific learning activities, not the technology.
- Design for changing needs – flexibility and adaptability is important.

Designing or altering the internal layout of a LRC is constrained by the space available. But there are several other factors to consider such as:

- the shape of the building and rooms, usual entrances, exits and emergency exits
- the position of light switches
- the accessibility of cabling and power sockets
- the number, size and position of the windows
- the acoustics of the rooms, and the effect of noise levels on users
- the size and nature of the stock and equipment
- the number of learning resource staff
- the number and types of potential users
- users' diverse learning styles – individual or group learning?
- the curriculum requirements and learning demands of subject departments
- the proximity of facilities such as toilets, refreshments and other student recreational zones
- the college pattern of open and closed hours.

Probably the best method of getting some new ideas on design and layout is to visit other similar LRCs and talk to managers to find out how they solved problems in their institution. Contact Information Services at CILIP for suggestions of examples of good practice and innovative design, and keep an eye on the CoFHE website.

LRCs are people-oriented environments. Therefore certain design features are essential, such as comfortable seating, some natural as well as artificial light and the attractive use of colour in decoration. For excellent detailed advice on design and layout, see the UfI booklet *Design for Learning*.[8] Here is a relevant reminder from this document:

Learning centres can create the right environment and project the right image with the design and layout of their centre. The design and layout can also communicate the wrong message and alienate people. Whatever you do (or do not do) you will project some kind of image and message.

4.5   Furnishings and equipment

The following is a list of the minimum requirements in furnishing and equipping a LRC, but of course the range of equipment will partly depend on the range of learning activities taking place. Detailed data recommendations are to be found in the list of design specifics at the end of this section.

Minimum requirements for furniture and shelving are to provide:

- ergonomic study carrels and/or tables with seats
- computer workstations with adjustable seats
- service desks and office furniture with adjustable seats
- some comfortable seating for relaxed reading
- flexible shelving systems
- mobile partitioning or screens
- display boards
- visual signage.

Minimum requirements for communication systems are to provide:

- a telephone
- a fax service
- e-mail and internet access
- connectivity for all users and LR staff to the college intranet, VLE and MLE.

Minimum requirements for security systems are to provide:

- a stock security system
- secure staff work space.

Minimum requirements for management systems are to provide:

- a library management system for operations control and monitoring
- interoperability between the library management system and other internal and external data or information systems.

Minimum requirements for ICT and ILT equipment are to provide:

- multimedia workstations with software applications, internet access, CD rewriter, CD-ROM and DVD capability
- systems for anti-virus control, copyright control and control of the misuse of computers
- laptop points.

Minimum requirements for audiovisual and presentation technology are to provide:

- video and audio tape playback equipment
- OHP and multimedia projection equipment.

Minimum requirements for reprographic services are to provide:

- mono and colour photocopiers
- a scanner
- mono and colour printers, laminator and binder.

Recommendations for the number of individual study and computer spaces were made several years ago by the Department of Education and Science (1983)[9] and the Follett Report (Joint Funding Council, 1993).[10] The suggested number of study spaces was 1 seat per 10 students FTE in FE and 1 seat per 6 students FTE in HE.

Results from the college survey show that there is a very wide variation in the number of study spaces: the minimum number was 2 and the maximum 404, with a median figure of 100 for all sizes of colleges. The survey results indicate that there should be at least 1 study space per 90 students.

The recommendation on the ratio of PCs to students from the FEFC (1999)[11] was 1 internet-enabled PC per 5 students at peak times. However, the survey results showed a wide diversity in the number of PCs with internet access available in LRCs, ranging from 0 to 384, with the median figure being 27. The number of computers bore no relationship to the number of students at the college.

These *Guidelines* recommend that there should be a minimum of 1 open access PC per 100 students.

Results from the college survey show that some LRCs are equipped with a high level of learning technology. Electronic whiteboards and facilities such as video-conferencing or wireless systems are increasingly available in learning centres. Certainly, continued advances in technology will require learning centres to keep up with current industry standards. *The SCONUL Vision* (2003) makes the point that as network capacity increases learners expect direct access to information resources from homes, offices and other locations, via a wide range of client devices. However, 'new types of e-book devices and handheld PCs connected through wireless networks to information resources within the library will shift the balance of PC provision and provide new opportunities for imaginative use of space'.[12]

4.6 Inclusiveness

The term 'inclusiveness' refers to targeted or under-represented groups, for example, those on low incomes or the unemployed, ethnic minorities, people with learning difficulties or disabilities, mature students, and young people with behavioural difficulties.

These groups will increasingly form a significant proportion of the post-compulsory student population. Catering for the needs of such diverse groups will have an effect on the interior design of buildings, which will in turn influence the design of LRCs.

The set of key questions listed in the FEDA Report *Equality Assurance*[13] is a useful tool in assessing whether a learning resource centre is accessible to a wide variety of users. For further detail in these guidelines, turn to Chapter 5.

Part IV of the Disability Discrimination Act (DDA) now requires all colleges to comply with its legal statements and LRMs have to be able to demonstrate that they have made reasonable adjustments to the physical features of their facilities to allow access by all types of users. The following is a list of recommendations; fuller information can be obtained from TechDis (see Glossary) about specialized learning aids and equipment appropriate for students with learning difficulties and/or physical disabilities.

- Main entrances and exits should be easy to access, with a ramp where necessary.
- Doors should be automatic or at least light to open; door handles should be at the right height for disabled users; vinyl stickers should be placed on any glass panels and clearly labelled Push/Pull.
- Floors should be covered in anti-slip material and free of obstructions.
- All signs should be clearly visible and easy to read, with pictograms and symbols as well as text, preferably using Arial font and in a large size.
- The issue and/or enquiry desks should be the right height for staff to work at and at least one desk should allow wheelchair users to reach the counter.
- In decoration there should be contrasting tones between the wall, the floor and other features; the tread and riser on stairs should be marked.
- Power and data cables should be above floor level.

- Some desks should be facing the middle of the room, not facing the wall, to aid deaf users.
- 1200 mm is the recommended minimum for circulation gangway space, 1800 mm preferred; 1200 mm is the minimum for space between shelving in order to allow wheelchair turning and 1000 mm is the minimum for access to a user's desk or workstation.
- Each user of a study space or workstation should have a minimum of 600 mm private space outwards from the desk.
- Desks and workstations should be a minimum of 1200 mm wide and 800 mm deep.
- The top of computer screens should be at eye level and document holders and foot rests should be available.

There is a number of briefing papers from CILIP on the provision of library and information services for disabled or disadvantaged users; these are available on the CILIP website.

4.7   Health and safety

Learning resource managers must be familiar with current health and safety legislation; a full list can be found in the DfES document *Key Design Guidance for Schools* (2003).[14] The key statutes are the Management of Health and Safety at Work Regulations 1992, including amendments 1994 and 1999, and the Workplace (Health, Safety and Welfare) Regulations, 1992, for staff employees. Compliance with these laws is a statutory and a professional requirement. Familiarity and compliance with one's own college health and safety policies and procedures will also be required.

All employers must assess all hazards present within the workplace, together with their associated levels of risk. Assessment of workplace hazards and risks should encompass provisions and stipulations within current health and safety regulations. For example, Manual Handling Operation Regulations 1992, Health and Safety (Display Screen Equipment) Regulations 1992 and Control of Substances Hazardous to Health Regulations (COSHH) 1994 will all have implications for learning resource managers, their staff and their users.

Risk assessments need not be undertaken by a 'safety expert' but must be completed to 'adequate' or 'suitable and sufficient' levels. Elements of risk assessment may therefore be delegated to service or line managers. The recommended document to use is *The Five Steps to Risk Assessment* issued by the Health and Safety Executive. It is important to document the findings of risk assessment inspections; steps must be taken to remove or minimize risk of injury or ill health from significant hazards and follow-up actions recorded. Risk assessments should be reviewed annually or when it is suspected that previous assessments are no longer valid. Planning for special projects (for instance stock re-location or reorganization), may also require risk assessments together with follow-up actions to minimize or remove potential hazards.

LRCs have developed as welcoming and informal places where the emphasis is on providing good access for users; inevitably there will be conflict between these principles and the imposition of rules and regulations for security. However, the value of stock and IT equipment makes security a necessary consideration. A reasonable level of staffing and supervision will deter thefts, but clear sightlines from staff desks and an electronic alarm system for stock are essential.

A LRM has a duty of care as an employer to his or her employees and health and safety must be not only included in staff induction but also regularly updated by training sessions for all learning resource staff. These aspects of security, affecting LRS staff, should be considered:

- Increasing numbers of users of college buildings, both from within college and without, require monitoring and supervision; LRS staff may be particularly vulnerable if working in the evening or at weekends when parts of the building may be quiet and unattended.
- LRS staff will need adequate support and protection in the event of challenging behaviour by users.
- Cash handling is also a security risk for LRS staff, particularly during non-standard working hours.

Possible ways of achieving some degree of protection for staff include using personal alarms, surveillance cameras, CCTV or mirrors, emergency telephone numbers and security staff. In particular, college security staff should be informed about any member of staff working alone in the evenings or at non-standard times. A report of any serious incident should be made to Student Services, the relevant tutor and the safety officer.

LRS staff should be aware of institutional policies and any associated documentation such as student charters or contracts, codes of conduct, grievance and disciplinary procedures. Any discipline problems in the LRC should be dealt with in accordance with these policies and with the support of the appropriate line manager.

4.8   Inspection and assessment

In England LRMs are advised to study the *Handbook for Inspecting Colleges* produced by OFSTED[15] in order to prepare themselves for inspection. Of the seven key assessment questions, the third is the one that affects the LRS, and inspectors must evaluate 'the adequacy, suitability and use of specialist

equipment, learning resources and accommodation'. The inspectors will judge
the quality of resource provision by considering the extent to which:

**accommodation provides a suitable setting for good teaching, training and learning,
and support for learners; learners have access to learning resources that are
appropriate for effective independent study; learners work in a healthy and safe
environment; resources are used to best effect in promoting learning; learning
resources and accommodation allow all learners to participate fully, regardless of
their gender, race, ethnicity, or learning difficulty or disability.**

The guidance on assessment details issues which specifically relate to learning
resources and these include whether there is enough space, whether the layout is
good and whether there are a quiet study area, accessibility to the internet and
controls on its use.

Although no objective standards or measures are given for assessing the
quality of learning resource provision, inspectors are provided with some
characteristics illustrating judgements about the effects of resources on the
quality of learning. Very good or excellent characteristics include:

**Libraries and learning resource centres are well designed, well equipped and well
used. They bring together a wide range of learning resources. Students and staff have
good access to modern computers, which are available in open-access areas and in
many classrooms and workshops. The college has supported its investment in
hardware and software with policies that encourage the use of computers . . . . All
areas of the college have easy access for students with restricted mobility.
Adaptations to classrooms, workplaces and workshops enable students with a wide
range of learning difficulties and physical disabilities to study effectively.**

Good or satisfactory characteristics do not mention libraries or learning centres,
but include the following:

**The accommodation for student services is spacious, it is adequately staffed, and it
offers students easy access to guidance materials . . . . Students and staff can use
modern computers, offering a wide range of software and good access to the Internet.
The quality of teaching accommodation and resources at out centres varies, but most
is good. Most areas of the college are accessible to students with restricted mobility.**

Characteristics indicating unsatisfactory resources do not mention libraries or learning centres but include the following:

Insufficient books, videos and computer-based learning materials to meet the needs of students; important areas of the college are inaccessible or unsuitable for students with learning difficulties and/or disabilities.

Learning resource provision for higher education students in higher education colleges or within further education will be assessed as part of subject or course reviews as before.

PI 1 **Ratio floor space : students**	**1m^2 : 10 students**
PI 2 **Ratio study spaces : students**	**1 : 90 students**
PI 3 **Ratio of open access internet ready computers : students**	**1 : 100**

References

1 Resource, *Better Public Libraries*, Resource (now MLA), 2003.

2 Bryson, J., Usherwood, R. and Proctor, R., *Libraries Must Also be Buildings? New library impact study*, Department of Information Studies, University of Sheffield, 2003.

3 Further Education Funding Council, *Guidance on Floorspace Management in Further Education Colleges: supplement to circular 97/37*, FEFC, 1997.

4 Chartered Institute of Library and Information Professionals, *UK Survey of Library and Learning Resource Provision in Further Education Colleges*, CILIP, 2003.

5 McDonald, A., *Space Requirements for Academic Libraries and Learning Resource Centres*, SCONUL (1996).

6 Mitchell, D. J. (ed.) *Library Design: principles and practice for the college librarian*, CoFHE, 1992.

7 Mitchell, D. J. (ed.) *Belfast '96 Designs on Learning: proceedings of the CoFHE annual study conference held at Stranmillis College, Belfast, 1st–4th April 1996*, CoFHE, 1997.

8 University for Industry, *Design for Learning*, UfI, 2003, www.ufi.com/designforlearning/000.htm.

9 Department of Education and Science, *Area Guidelines for Sixth Form, Tertiary and NAFE Colleges: design note 33*, DES, 1983.

10 Joint Funding Council's Libraries Review Group: *Report: a report for the HEFCE, SHEFC, HEFCW and DENI* (The Follett Report), HEFCE, 1993.

11 Further Education Funding Council, *Networking Lifelong Learning: an ILT development strategy for FE*, FEFC, 1999.

12 Society of College, National and University Libraries, *The SCONUL Vision*, SCONUL, 2003.

13 Dadzie, S., *Equality Assurance: self-assessment for equal opportunities in further education*, FEDA, 1998.

14 Department for Education and Skills, *Key Design Guidance for Schools*, DfES, 2003.

15 OFSTED, *Handbook for Inspecting Colleges*, OFSTED, 2001.

4.9 Appendix: Design specifics

The following data may assist in determining the environmental requirements of a learning resource centre.

Allocation of college space[1]
The total area for further education college learning resource centres should be:

- at least 10% of total college area or
- a minimum of 20% of the total teaching space.

Load bearing structure[2]
The load bearing capacity of the floor housing books stacks must exceed minimum strength of 6.5 kN/m^2.

Light[3]
50% daylight is recommended, but the glare of the sun must be cut out.

Lighting[4]
The Department for Education and Employment states that:

- Work surfaces should receive minimum illumination of 300 Lux but dimming is recommended.
- Light fittings should produce a glare index no higher than 19.
- To keep VDU screen reflections under control, use CIBSE category 2 lighting (see Glossary) incorporating low brightness louvered fluorescent fittings.

Heating[5]
The minimum temperature should be 18°C when the external air temperature is –1°C.

Ventilation[6]
There should be:

- minimum ventilation of at least 3 litres of fresh air per second per occupant
- the capability of providing at least 8 litres of fresh air per second per occupant on very hot days
- natural ventilation where possible; mechanical methods should be draught free.

Study space
There should be:

- 1 seat per 10 students FTE in further education[7]
- 1 seat per 6 students FTE in higher education[8]
- 2.5 m^2 per student workspace in resource based learning rooms or learning resource centres[9]
- between 2.5 m^2 and 4 m^2 per student workspace in higher education[10]
- reader modules minimum 900 mm x 600 mm[11]
- ICT or ILT spaces minimum 1200 mm (preferably 1400 mm.) x 800 mm[12]
- circulation space (gangways) of 1200 mm minimum (1800 mm preferred); access to desk or workstation requires 1000 mm minimum; private space for user 600 mm outward from the desk.[13]

References

1 Further Education Funding Council, *Guidance on Floorspace Management in Further Education Colleges: supplement to circular 97/37*, FEFC, 1997.

2 McDonald, A., *Moving Your Learning Resource Service*, Aslib, 1994.

3 Rogers, L., New British Libraries: sector report learning resource centres, *Royal Institute of British Architects: Interiors*, October 1995.

4 Department for Education and Employment, *Structural Requirements and Health And Safety: circular no.10/96*, DfEE, 1996.

5 Department for Education and Employment, ibid.

6 Department for Education and Employment, ibid.

7 Department of Education and Science, *Area Guidelines for Sixth Form, Tertiary and NAFE Colleges: design note 33*, DES, 1983.

8 Joint Funding Councils' Libraries Review Group, *Report: a report for the HEFCE, SHEFC, HEFCW and DENI (Follett)*, HEFC, 1993.

9 Further Education Funding Council, *Accommodation Strategies: guidance for colleges: supplement to circular 97/19*, FEFC, 1997.

10 McDonald, A., *Space Requirements for Academic Libraries and Learning Resource Centres*, SCONUL, 1996.

11 Joint Funding Councils' Libraries Review Group, op. cit.

12 Joint Funding Councils' Libraries Review Group, op. cit.

13 University for Industry, *Design for Learning*, UfI, 2003.

5

Accessibility

R7
Learning resource services need to be accessible to all students, including those with learning disabilities and difficulties, distance learners and those who may feel socially excluded from further education.

The learning resource service must be accessible to the whole college community and offer a welcoming, friendly and supportive environment. It must cater for a diverse population in terms of age, ability, mode of study, and teaching and learning styles.

A growing number of students in further and higher education are not studying full-time. Social inclusion means an increasing number of students with a range of learning needs will form a significant part of the college population. Anti-discriminatory legislation such as part IV of the Disability Discrimination Act 1995 (DDA), or, as it is also referred to, the Special Educational Needs and Disability Act 2001 (SENDA), and the Race Relations (Amendment) Act 2000 (RRA) ensure all students must have equality of access to all resources and services. It is essential that services are flexible enough to cater for their demands. All students, irrespective of their mode of study or ability are entitled to the full range of services offered. Senior managers must ensure that the LRS is responsive to the needs of all students.

5.1 Opening hours

This diversity of the student population means students may not be able to or wish to visit LRCs during the traditional 9–5 opening hours. Many colleges now offer courses throughout the vacation and the increase of students on open and flexible learning courses brings demand for more flexible opening hours.

Another issue is that resources may be held in closed collections, such as departmental collections only accessible to certain students at certain times. These guidelines recommend that such collections are held in central locations equally accessible to all.

The CILIP survey of further education (see Chapter 4) reveals that 64% of main site libraries are open for more than 50 hours per week in term, providing a service in the evening and, in some cases, on Saturday. Out of term time this figure drops to 29% of libraries open more than 40%. Some 14% of libraries close at vacation periods. Consideration should be given to:

- the learning resource centre being open all the hours the college is open
- offering weekend and vacation opening
- having qualified and adequately trained staff available at all times to assist users with their information needs.

These guidelines recommend that LRCs are open for a minimum of 50 hours per week in term.

5.2   Electronic access

The SFEFC (2003)[1] self-evaluation toolkit provides recommendations for managing and accessing electronic resources. When planning electronic services managers should consider:

- the suitability of learning resource management systems to permit interoperability with other systems
- cataloguing standards such as MARC21
- metadata standards.

All students should have full access to the full range of electronic services. This includes having access to:

- the catalogue for searching, renewals and reservation purposes
- online databases and datasets
- digitized articles and books
- themed web links or virtual library
- an electronic enquiry service.

Resources should be available on and off campus through an authentication service such as Athens in line with licensing agreements. Students also require support in accessing and using electronic resources. This may take the form of:

- induction and information skills and literacy programmes delivered in the learning resource centre
- induction and information skills and literacy programmes available electronically through MLE or VLE
- online tools such as Netskills, TONIC, JISC Resource Discovery Network and Virtual Training Suite
- user guides and instructional tools in print and electronic format
- use of web pages
- staff who are skilled in supporting students using online resources.

5.3 Distance learners

The LRS needs to be flexible to respond to the needs of distance learners. Support for these students may be given by allowing or providing:

- online registration, reservations and renewals
- a postal loans service
- a photocopying service under CLA agreements
- remote access to subscription databases and datasets, e-books and articles
- an enquiry or help desk by telephone or e-mail
- user guides and leaflets
- online induction and information skills programmes
- a VLE.

5.4 Equal opportunities

LRMs must ensure that all students have equal access to services and resources. Services must now be proactive in anticipating the needs of various student groups. Clear policies and procedures on equality of access should be in place and widely available in a variety of formats. Staff who are fully aware of and trained in equality and inclusiveness issues are best able to support the various groups. The Museums, Libraries and Archives Council best practice manual,[2] MLA toolkits[4] and FEDA *Equality Assurance* (1998)[3] provide useful guidance and tools to provide equality of access and promote equal opportunities.

Addressing language diversity is an important consideration in all colleges and efforts should be made to provide appropriate materials for all language groups. This is particularly so in Wales where inspectors are looking specifically for bilingual provision.

5.5   Disability

Under the DDA it is unlawful for a disabled student to be treated less favourably than others because of their disability. Colleges must also take 'reasonable steps' to ensure that disabled students are not placed at a disadvantage compared with non-disabled students.

LRSs have a responsibility to make facilities available to students with learning difficulties or disabilities. The Museums, Libraries and Archives Council (MLA)[4] provides useful advice and toolkits for ensuring services are accessible:

- Access should be level.
- There should be lifts between floors and levels.
- OPACs, ICT/ILT and audiovisual equipment should be adapted for visually and hearing impaired users.
- Counters, service points, study desks and ICT and ILT workstations should be of suitable height to accommodate users in wheelchairs or with other mobility difficulties.
- There should be enough room for circulation and turning of wheelchairs and spinal carriages.
- There should be a loop system and text phone system for the hearing impaired.
- Signs and guiding should be tactile where possible.
- There should be good acoustics.
- Fire alarms should be visible as well as audible.
- Properly adapted toilets should be provided.
- Floor covering should be non-slip.
- Passages should kept clear.
- Signs and guiding should be mixed case in plain typeface.
- Books should not be shelved too high or too low.

In providing access to resources for disabled students consideration should be given to:

- the range of resources
- use of services such as interlibrary loan systems
- use of services provided by groups and bodies such as the RNIB
- provision of assistive technologies
- ensuring staff are trained in supporting the user in accessing assistive technology
- providing user guides and leaflets in a variety of formats, large print, disk, audiotape and web-based

- ensuring all web pages meet an accessibility standard such as W3C
- extended loan periods and reservation holding times
- providing an online catalogue screen with text that may be magnified and have speech output facility
- colour and layout of guides and leaflets
- lower photocopying charges for visually impaired users
- book retrieval services
- designated borrowers for students unable to access the centre because of disability
- individual inductions and information skills sessions.

5.6 Widening participation and social inclusion

LRSs have a role in promoting cultural diversity and equality of opportunity. Social inclusion has introduced groups of students who may suffer from lack of confidence, low self-esteem and self-consciousness. LRSs can do much to support such students by:

- providing a welcoming and attractive environment
- ensuring staff are friendly and helpful and have good communication skills
- having attractive and hard-wearing furniture and equipment
- encouraging users to become more independent by having clear and concise signs and guidance
- displaying posters and guides that reflect cultural diversity
- providing leaflets in different languages.

PI 4	
Opening hours	**Minimum of 50 hours per week in term-time**

References

1   Scottish Further Education Funding Council, *Resources and Services Supporting Learning: a service development quality toolkit*, SFEFC, 2003.

2   The Museums, Libraries and Archives Council, *Access for All Toolkit: enabling inclusion for museums, libraries and archives*, MLA, 2004.

3   Further Education Development Agency, *Equality Assurance: self-assessment for equal opportunities in further education*, FEDA. 1998.

4   The Museums, Libraries and Archives Council (then Resource) has produced the following toolkits: *Access to Museums, Archives and Libraries for Disabled Users: self-assessment toolkit 1*, Resource, 2003; *Library Services for Visually Impaired People: a manual of best practice*, Resource, 2000; (with Asdal Institute) *Self-assessment Toolkit: cultural diversity for museums, libraries and archives*, Resource, 2003.

6

Learning materials

Learning materials must reflect teaching, learning and information needs of staff and students. The range of learning materials available may take many forms, so the use of the word 'collection' or 'stock' does not refer only to print-based materials. Learning materials should be provided in a variety of formats and styles in order to cater for specific groups.

6.1 Size of collection

The LRS must be given an appropriate level of funding annually to enable its collection to reach and maintain the levels of stock necessary to support the curriculum and to enable the purchase of new material to replenish, update and improve stock.

The size of the collection will be further influenced by the:

- number of students
- number of LRCs
- proportion of advanced and higher level work
- proportion of part-time students in the college
- range of the curriculum

- decisions made as to whether to hold stock or to provide access to collections elsewhere and/or in electronic form
- resources provided in other areas of the institution
- modes of course delivery, including MLEs and VLEs
- storage capacity of the LRC.

6.2   Collection development

The stock development policy should be based on the information needs and the information strategy of the institution. This policy should specifically address the adequacy of subject cover, which is the primary source of user satisfaction. Other factors include:

- provision for new and existing courses
- provision of a range of materials catering for students at different levels of ability and learning styles
- provision of lending and reference materials
- provision of electronic resources
- provision of general and recreational reading material for staff and students
- the price of material in different media
- the price of material in different disciplines
- loss and/or replenishment rates.

6.3   Collection management

The LRS needs to develop a stock management policy. This policy should identify methods of measuring stock performance in order that decisions can be made about:

- the organization of material – cataloguing, classification and inputting subject headings (or keywords)
- the relevance of current holdings
- where, and how, financial resources should be targeted
- the disposal of materials that have lost their relevance
- the provision of web-based resources for e-learning.

A discussion of this topic can be found in the *Library Association Record* article of February 1998, 'Get to know your stock', by George Kerr,[1] and *Collection Management in Academic Libraries* edited by Clare Jenkins and Mary Morley.[2]

In forming a stock management policy consideration should be given to the following:

- *Statistical data*. Data on stock use will provide information that the LRM, in liaison with teaching staff, can use to make appropriate choices of materials for the collection. These materials can, subsequently, be included on recommended resource lists.
- *Relevance*. The relevance of materials to the courses provided by the institution and the ability of these materials to be exploited across disciplines should be the key element in their initial purchase. The criteria for stock editing should be based on the ability of the resources to meet the needs of users based on professional judgement, currency, usage, shelf space and input from teaching staff.
- *Replacement*. The LRS will require a rolling programme of stock replacement. However, in some subjects such as computing, law and medicine, the replacement rate will be faster as information in these subjects changes more quickly. Worn, damaged and obsolescent stock should be replaced regularly.
- *Stock auditing*. A regular programme of stock checks should be established to assess loss and inconsistency. This may be an obligation required by auditors. It has the enhanced benefit of maintaining the currency of the stock and ensuring the accuracy of the catalogue. Heavy losses may indicate the need for improving security measures. Stockchecks should be carried out electronically to eliminate incorrect data on the LMS.

6.4 Electronic resources

In *Building an Electronic Resource Collection: a practical guide*[3] Stuart Lee and Frances Boyle state that electronic resources: 'should be considered alongside printed resources . . . and that libraries should formulate an overall "coherent" collection development policy covering all material' (p.9). The same principles of stock development and management apply but there are other aspects to take into consideration:

- licensing terms allowing networking of the resource or restricting the number of concurrent users
- remote access to the resource
- limited access to archives
- free or JISC subsidized resources
- the duration (and possible rising costs) of licences.

6.5 Security

In order to protect stock and to ensure that losses are kept to a minimum, security measures should be carefully considered. Appropriate measures should be taken to secure equipment and guard against theft and damage in learning resource centres. Possible measures include barcoding, ownership stamps, infra-red security marks, postcode branding, electronic tagging, lockable display cases, equipment clamps and chains.

The LRS should have a disaster recovery plan in order to secure material and provide access to resources in the event of a disaster.

PI 5	
Ratio of books : students	**3 : 1**
PI 6	
Ratio of AV material : students	**1 : 10**
PI 7	
Ratio of periodical titles : students	**1 : 100**

References

1   Kerr, G., Get to Know Your Stock, *Library Association Record*, **100** (2), February 1998, 78–81.
2   Jenkins, C. and Morley, M. (eds), *Collection Management in Academic Libraries*, Gower, 1999.
3   Lee, S. and Boyle, F., *Building an Electronic Resource Collection: a practical guide*, 2nd edn, Facet Publishing, 2004.

7

Human resources

LRS staff make a core contribution to learning in further and higher education. They are responsible for supplying open access learning facilities, information and curriculum resources to their users, together with associated services. They manage and operate a major educational facility and its systems and procedures. This chapter will consider the staffing implications and recommendations for a college LRS.

7.1 The contribution of learning resources service staff to learning and teaching

The principal ways in which the staff contribute are by:

- managing resources for learning, information and maximizing access and availability
- identifying and providing a diverse range of resources appropriate to students' curriculum needs; in addition, providing expertise and advice on selection of resources to teaching staff
- designing and managing systems of control and retrieval for resources; traditionally this has meant cataloguing, classification and indexing, but

increasingly it is about issues such as control of web-based resources, metadata management and provision for e-learning

- designing and managing both physical and electronic environments for independent learning
- mediating between learners and information resources; LRS staff have a key role as learning facilitators or enablers, working to support students in their learning outside the classroom
- teaching transferable information, learning or knowledge navigation skills; these are core enabling skills for independent and lifelong learning
- supporting the development, implementation and success of strategies for mixed-mode and blended learning at various levels, in order to improve access and choice for students, to serve remote areas and to compete in wider markets.

7.2   Responsibilities of learning resource service staff

Within this context of the learning environment, it is the responsibility of the LRM and LRS staff to ensure that:

- physical and electronic learning environments are conducive to learning in a variety of modes and styles
- services are inclusive, and accessible to learners with a variety of needs and circumstances
- users are given an appropriate induction to the LRS and provided with professional enquiry and information services
- there are close links between the LRS and teaching staff and senior management to support the curriculum and to provide an information literacy programme
- LRC inventories are updated
- health and safety risk assessments are undertaken
- there is continuous development and improvement of services
- services are provided efficiently and cost-effectively
- the professional skills and knowledge of LRS staff are kept up to date.

Several of the responsibilities above are specifically included in OFSTED's *Handbook for Inspecting Colleges*.[1]

7.3   Staffing structure and qualifications

High calibre, well motivated and appropriately qualified and experienced staff are essential to ensure that the LRS team makes the fullest possible contribution to the goals of the college. The range of services provided by a LRS team means that an appropriate staffing structure needs to be in place, with staff appointed across a range of specialisms and skills. These will be in areas of library and information work, ICT, ILT or e-learning, learning support or teaching and maybe others. All posts should be graded according to the level of contribution that they make, the level of responsibility that they bear and the appropriate qualifications that they hold.

The different levels of post that the structure contains may include: LRM, deputy LRM and other professionally qualified posts such as assistant librarian, subject librarian, learning facilitator, paraprofessional or supervisory posts, front-line service delivery staff and trainee posts. For possible job titles and specifications, it is useful to refer to the vacancies listings in CILIP literature.

Staff who have professional responsibilities (such as managing staff and budgets and undertaking information skills training with groups of students) should have a recognized library and information qualification at higher level. They should be Chartered Members of CILIP, or candidates for registration. The use of professionally qualified and chartered librarians should be part of the quality assurance process. A Chartered Member will have:

- completed an approved course of study at graduate or postgraduate level
- undergone a period of workplace training followed by the submission of evidence of professional skills
- signed a Code of Professional Conduct which commits them to be competent in their professional activities and to keep their skills and knowledge up to date
- demonstrated a commitment to continuing professional development
- involvement in a professional network which continually develops professional practice.

As a library professional's role will include some instruction of students, a teaching or learning support qualification is also desirable. Other desirable qualifications are a subject degree, IT or management qualification. Staff who are responsible for the technical or ICT aspects of a LRS team should have appropriate advanced qualifications or be working towards them, as this area of work requires increasing expertise.

LRS assistants should be appropriately qualified, for example with a S/NVQ 2 or 3 in Information and Library Services (or work towards it) and/or an appropriate IT qualification such as the European Computer Driving Licence.

The CILIP website (www.cilip.org.uk) contains specific information about library and information qualifications at all levels; a new framework of qualifications is currently in production. The salary guides for further and higher education (2002)[2] provide more detail about possible staffing structures.

7.4 Staffing roles and functions

The LRM should be a chartered librarian and have a status on a par with middle managers within the college. However, results from CILIP's further education college survey (2003)[3] indicate that there is considerable diversity in the status of the library manager at the 276 colleges who responded to this question. There were 67.4% who described themselves as middle managers, but only 19.2% described themselves as head of department. Direct access to senior management of the college was only possible in four cases, suggesting that the library had to rely on non-library staff to represent their case with the main decision-making body of the college.

The major areas of responsibility of the role include:

- integration of the service with all other managerial and academic components and processes of the institution
- planning, development, direction and promotion of the service
- overall management of all the resources – human, financial, physical, electronic – which comprise the service
- advising on the resource requirements of the service and preparation of budgets
- establishing and reviewing a comprehensive framework of policies, systems and procedures
- service evaluation and quality management
- ensuring service cost-effectiveness
- ensuring mechanisms are in place for regular meetings, staff development and appraisal
- positioning the service in the wider local, regional and national information world
- informing senior management of opportunities for developing the contribution of the learning resource service.

In larger institutions, there may be one or more deputy or assistant librarians at second or third levels of responsibility. A senior management team will normally share the above responsibilities, but ultimate responsibility remains with the head or manager. The CILIP further education college survey (2003)[3] assumed that the library manager would have an overview of all activities, only taking responsibility for a few particular tasks; however, a significant number of responses indicated that the LRM was undertaking all levels of library management activity.

Developments in resource-based or ICT-, ILT-mediated learning mean that learning resource staff work increasingly as members of cross-professional learning and teaching teams. Many staff are required to adopt flexible work patterns in order to meet demands for enhanced access to services.

The allocation of the roles and responsibilities for team members will depend on the size of the learning centre(s) and range of services provided. Typically the functions will include:

1 Working with users through:
   - academic liaison and communications
   - learner support and learning facilitation
   - information and enquiry services
   - frontline service delivery – reception, lending services, booking systems, record updating, ICT and ILT support, rota management
   - supervision and discipline of users
   - learning support and assisting users with special needs
   - current awareness information for users
   - information, learning or research skills teaching

2 Working with learning materials and learning facilities through:
   - collection management and development
   - acquisition of learning and information resources
   - cataloguing, classification and indexing of learning materials
   - document delivery, including external document delivery (interlibrary loans)
   - development and management of resource-based and open and distance learning materials and facilities
   - electronic and online materials and facilities
   - special collections for subject areas or groups of users
   - promotional displays and features
   - audiovisual and media services
   - technician services
   - copyright and rights management

3 Managing systems through:
   - LMS maintenance and development
   - intranet and internet management and development
   - security compliance and authentication systems
   - signs and guiding
   - financial management and control
   - performance data collection and analysis
   - records management for auditing purposes
   - health and safety management
   - administrative and secretarial services

4 Working with staff through:

- collaborative working, both with learning resources staff and other players in the team
- team leadership, section management and team performance reviews
- staff management – induction, training, development and review

These functions cannot be simply deemed appropriate for particular job levels as there will be a considerable range of expertise required to suit different contexts; the larger the team the more likely it is that staff will specialize in what they do. Generally speaking the management functions should be allocated to professionally qualified staff, because of their qualifications and experience. Clear lines of responsibility for different functions should be worked out in any team and well-planned training and procedures should be set up for all jobs.

7.5   Staffing levels and salary scales

The OFSTED *Handbook for Inspecting Colleges* (2002)[1] does consider the effect of staffing levels on students' learning. For example, inspectors will look at 'whether there is a sufficient number of adequately qualified technical and other support staff to help students and teachers, and to maintain resources and learning materials'.

Results from the CILIP further education college survey (2003)[3] across the UK show that the median staffing levels in college libraries conceal a wide variation in actual staffing levels in colleges of a similar size. Thus, for a small college of up to 8000 students, the number ranged from 2 to 25, with a median of 5 staff. For a medium college of up to 18,000 students, the range was from 2 to 48, with a median of 10 staff. For a large college, the range was from 7 to 46 with a median of 16. The figures for HE colleges show that in 2002 out of 57 colleges the mean number of library staff was 20.

These figures are not recommended staffing levels; they do not take into account, for instance, the higher staffing levels required if there are several college sites and library desks that need staff coverage. The number of staff required will be determined by such factors as the size of the institution, the style of curriculum delivery, the range of services provided by the learning centre(s), access times convenient to users, the need to maintain managerial and developmental activities, as well as frontline service, and to maintain the quality of the learning environment to agreed levels of service.

Results from the further education college survey (2003)[3] showed that the number of qualified librarians for all sizes of college across the UK ranged from 0 to 17. In some cases, librarians were working during term-time only or part-time. For small colleges, the median number of qualified staff was 1; for medium-sized colleges, the median was 2 and for large colleges the median was 4.

The median figure for HE colleges from LISU Library and Information statistics tables 2002 was 7.8 qualified staff.[4] A number of libraries in different areas of the UK have a median figure of 1 qualified librarian for more than 10,500 students; the number for higher education colleges is 1 per 436 FTE students.

These guidelines are recommending the following ratios for staffing:

FTE learning resource staff : students   1 : 1000
(excluding ICT support staff)
FTE professional staff : students   1 : 5000

There should be a similar ratio (1 : 5000 students) for designated ICT support staff (in addition to the figures above for LRS staff). These staffing figures make no special allowance for multi-site operations. The CILIP further education college survey[3] found that it is rare for libraries to have specialized ICT staff, except in the north east, where 46% of college libraries have full-time ICT staff. ICT problems are dealt with either by library staff themselves or the library must take its turn alongside other demands on ICT staff throughout the college. This lack of ICT staff means that librarians spend an increasing amount of time on ICT problems and it is a distinct drawback to the efficiency of the online learning environment.

The recommendation from CILIP on the question of salary levels is that all library posts should be paid according to the levels of responsibility, qualifications and experience they require. Salaries should also be on a par with colleagues within the institution with similar levels of responsibility. The LRM should have a salary on the college management spine and the same conditions of service as other college academic managers. Other professional library staff may also have academic, managerial or technical responsibilities and should be paid accordingly, with no less than £18,000 paid to those who are chartered. Libraries need to be able to attract and retain professional staff, so their pay structures should reflect national pay scales.

The CILIP further and higher education salary guides (2002)[2] give recommended pay scales for the various levels of library staff. These guidelines are regularly updated and are available on the CILIP website.

7.6   Staff training and development

It is the responsibility of the LRM to set up professional and efficiently organized systems for staff recruitment and selection, induction, training and development, and performance review. Within the institution there will be recognized procedures for human resource management, but the LRM will need to ensure that all these are planned and carried out properly for the benefit of the library and its staff. Human resource management textbooks and CILIP guides can be referred to for examples of good procedures and practice.

The induction and training of new staff is particularly important and should not be left to chance. There should be a formal induction programme, introducing the new member of staff to the institution and the learning environment as well as specific tasks, and this period of training should be backed up by the appointment of a mentor from the library team. Training may take some time – a full academic year will need to pass before LRS staff can be said to have experienced the full nature of academic learning resource work.

Regular group or team meetings are essential for good planning, communication and efficient operations, particularly when there is more than one LRC and common, unified methods of working are required. The OFSTED inspectors will be looking at and evaluating the range, quality and accessibility of resources across a college for the full range of students, so relevance, consistency and efficiency are a necessity for all learning resources staff. The quality of links between libraries and college departments will also be considered by inspectors. This aspect of inspection may be difficult to measure, but library staff will help themselves if they regularly discuss and document any links that have been made.

Staff training and development is essential to service quality and service development; one way of achieving this is to organize staff updating or training sessions as part of the regular meetings programme. Broad areas for skills and knowledge development appropriate for learning resource staff include:

- learning and teaching skills, including learner support and learning facilitation
- strategic and operational management training
- ICT and ILT skills and knowledge
- team-working and collaborative skills
- professional and technical skills in librarianship and learning resource management (for example cataloguing and classification, electronic and web-based resources management, enquiry and information services, subject specialisms)
- reception skills and customer care
- advice, guidance and counselling skills
- skills to deal with behavioural or disciplinary problems
- health and safety knowledge
- awareness of the wider policy issues affecting further and higher education and the information world.

All levels of learning resource staff, including part-timers, should have the opportunity to follow courses leading to appropriate qualifications, including library, teaching, technical or management qualifications, and to take part in external courses and in-service training. They should have access to the same practical support, including financial assistance and additional leave, as is available to colleagues in other departments. Para-professional and other technical or administrative staff should equally be included and encouraged to obtain appropriate qualifications.

CILIP has produced a framework for professional development to encourage members to review systematically the state of their knowledge and skills. It is based on the belief that continuing professional development is a responsibility of the individual working in partnership with their employer. The document encourages librarians to analyse their needs, develop a coherent CPD programme and record progress.

Staff training and development should be considered an integral part of a formal staff review or appraisal scheme. The college will probably have such a scheme organized and library managers will be obliged to follow the recognized procedures. Reviews should be carried out annually by line managers or appropriate learning resources staff and targets established for the individual for the coming year. These targets can be agglomerated by library managers to form group or team targets and action plans. They should cover individual training needs as well as institutionally driven training programmes. However, results from the CILIP further education college survey indicate that only 25% of library managers have a staff development budget; therefore 75% have no control over decisions concerning the appropriateness and timeliness of staff development activities.

LRS staff need to maintain formal and informal contacts with others working in the profession if they are to develop their contribution to the full. By participating in professional meetings, training events and conferences organized by CoFHE, UC&R, CILIP and other bodies, they will be able to keep abreast of new developments and learn best practice from their colleagues at other college libraries. This is particularly important in ILT and support for students where the pace of change makes so many demands on library staff to adapt to new technical systems and continually update their ILT skills.

PI 8
Ratio of FTE LRS staff : students   **1 : 1000**

PI 9
Ratio of FTE professional staff : students   **1 : 5000**

(There should be a similar ratio for designated FTE ICT support staff : students)

References

1   OFSTED, *Handbook for Inspecting Colleges*, OFSTED, 2001.

2   Chartered Institute of Library and Information Professionals, *Further Education and Higher Education Salary Guides*, CILIP, 2002.

3   Chartered Institute of Library and Information Professionals, *UK Survey of Library and Learning Resource Provision in Further Education Colleges*, CILIP, 2003.

4   Library and Information Statistics Unit, *Library and Statistics Tables*, LISU, 2002.

8

Finance

It is the LRM's responsibility to advise institutional management of the LRS's financial needs, prepare estimates and budgets, and control expenditure within agreed parameters.

An analysis of the type, level and cost of the learning resource service should be carried out during the strategic planning process. The college's expectations of that service should then be met with an appropriate level of funding rather than unrealistic historical allocations.

Resource management for LRMs generally means:

- an annual bid, based on estimates of need and previous budgets, for funds to buy materials and to cover operating and ongoing costs such as service and maintenance contracts, and network licence renewals
- a separate bid for capital equipment and associated maintenance costs
- periodic bids for posts to be added to the staffing establishment, or, if there are vacancies in an existing establishment, for the 'release' of the post for filling by permanent or temporary appointment
- occasional requests for more resources in other areas – most notably space
- allocation of the available resources between the various spending heads

(payroll, non-payroll, materials, operating costs, books, journals and other media)

- monitoring the rate of spend of the resources made available under each major heading in response to the various bids submitted
- producing an annual report and summary financial statement for senior management
- regular cost-cutting exercises, whether driven by a central directive that aims for a percentage reduction in projected spend or to maintain value for money
- periodic reviews of actual and potential capacity for income generation, within or outside the institution
- costing the resource implications of any new course provision
- costing any 'new build' learning resource provision.

LRS staff must ensure that resources are managed, and are seen to be managed, efficiently and effectively. The LRM should undertake an annual financial risk assessment exercise of learning resource provision in the college, covering aspects such as the implications of curriculum changes, depreciation, loss, maintenance agreements, LMS support costs, increasing subscription and consumables costs.

When estimating the cost of the service, the following factors need to be taken into consideration:

- general overheads – lighting, heating
- staff – salaries, on-costs (such as National Insurance contributions and pensions), training costs, time spent in specific activities
- curriculum demands and developments – levels of study, teaching and learning styles, student numbers, different disciplines and taught hours
- number of sites – duplication of equipment and materials
- materials purchase – new and replacement stock, range of resources, for example provision for hardcopy print material, audiovisual material and electronic resources
- subscriptions – periodicals, online resources
- depreciation – replacement of outdated, lost or non-returned resources
- furniture, fittings, equipment – developments in educational technology, requirements of learners with special needs, security systems, damage, wear and tear
- administration – stationery, postage, telephones, electronic communications, inter-learning resource service loans
- income generation – fines, photocopying, membership subscriptions, external services and sales of consumables.

8.1   Budget allocation

The LRS budget should be allocated annually. As there is a demand-led element to the allocation, the LRS budget may increase, or decrease, over the financial year, and may be affected by fluctuations of enrolment, retention and achievement rates, as controlled by the funding councils.

While the funding councils are the major providers of academic institutions' finance, a significant proportion of funds can be derived from other sources, for example, franchised or other collaborative courses, European funding, direct higher education funding to further education colleges, commercial courses or full cost courses. The learning resource service budget should reflect this diversity of income.

8.2   Managing the budget

The learning resource manager is accountable for the management of the budget and must be familiar with the parent institution's financial regulations.

The use of budget headings allows the learning resources manager to track expenditure. The finance department of the institution usually allocates headings, but even if it does, it is still wise for the learning resource manager to devise appropriate categories of expenditure.

LRMs will usually have the right to 'vire' funds from one heading to another. This means administering a 'bottom-line' budget, and transferring funds between headings if, and when, necessary. This can be useful in making scarce resources go further, and also in engendering a flexible approach towards resource management, particularly at a time of funding cutbacks. One way of protecting the budget from cutbacks would be to commit acquisitions early on in the year, for example, by paying in advance for standing orders and journal subscriptions.

By far the most complex part of the budget to manage, and the part whose results are most obvious to learning resource users, is the expenditure on acquisitions, that is the allocation of funds to different subject areas or academic departments, and types of material, for example, books, journals, CD-ROMS and electronic materials. It is therefore essential to involve curriculum, and other interested, staff in the allocation of library resources in order for the library to make use of subject knowledge of teaching staff and to ensure that courses are adequately and fairly funded. A model of devolved control of library budgets may be appropriate for purchasing resources or expenditure on subscriptions where teaching departments are allocated an amount of money with the actual purchasing of the resources managed by the learning resource service staff. An LRS run library committee would be a good vehicle for prioritizing expenditure and engaging teaching staff more in the selection and promotion of learning resources.

The management of the acquisitions budget includes monitoring the effectiveness of the spend (cost effectiveness), and analysing the patterns of expenditure. In doing so the LRM will take into account factors such as the type of material (for instance whether electronic, AV or print-based), usage, typical costs of material for that type of provision – some areas are traditionally more expensive to resource than others.

The use of tools such as spreadsheets, databases and acquisition modules will allow the monitoring of expenditure patterns to be carried out, and will help to make any necessary adjustments to expenditure. They will also allow the learning resource manager to provide the management of the institution with appropriate budget information on request. If changes to expenditure have to be made these need to be referred back to the operational plan and particularly to its objectives and performance targets.

Organizational politics have to be taken into account and, indeed, used to advantage in any approach to resource management within the learning resource service.

Success in managing resources is an art. It is an art of compromise, and rarely, if it is to be successful, one of confrontation. The successful manager has to be credible in terms of 'delivering the goods', however defined by the institution, and at whatever agreed costs.

8.3 Income generation

The LRS often assists the institution's income generation, for example by supporting the college's commercial activities.

In addition the LRS may engage directly in income generation by selling information services or facilities to external users, by hiring out facilities such as seminar and training rooms, by providing photocopiers and by selling such items as books, stationery and computer consumables.

Collecting fines for overdue materials is also a potential source of income; however, the main reason for fines is to encourage the circulation of stock. This income should be credited to the LRS and should not affect its base funding.

Any monies obtained by the college from students for the non-return of learning resources should be credited to the LRS in order to replace the lost items.

PI 10	
LRS budget (bookfund)	**£5 per student**

Conclusion

The purpose of these *Guidelines* is to describe how a learning resource service should operate. They are designed to be used flexibly and are not meant to be prescriptive although quantitative performance indicators have been reintroduced to give a base figure for minimum provision in a few key areas.

The *Guidelines* are intended to be comprehensive and look at learning resources in their entirety. However, the various sections are also, to a great extent, autonomous and can be applied as and when required. The *Guidelines* should therefore be viewed as guidance notes for those responsible for running learning resource services in the further education sector by providing them with the basis for making informed decisions.

These *Guidelines* continue the tradition of reflecting the diverse range and nature of the skills that exist among learning resource staff in further education. They reflect the fact that a learning resource service is more to do with the staff that work within it rather than the material resources it provides.

As always, the value of the *Guidelines*, and the learning resource services they aim to support, will be demonstrated by the satisfaction levels of those actually using learning resource services in further education.

Bibliography

Audit Commission, *Building Better Library Services*, Audit Commission, 2002.

Brophy, P., cited in Winkworth, I.,Quality Issues and Performance Indicators in Academic Libraries. In Spiller, D. (ed.), *Academic Library Surveys and Statistics in Practice*, LISU, 1998.

Bryson, J., Usherwood, R. and Proctor, R., *Libraries Must Also Be Buildings? New library impact study*, Department of Information Studies, University of Sheffield, 2003.

Chartered Institute of Library and Information Professionals, *Further Education and Higher Education Salary Guides*, CILIP, 2002.

Chartered Institute of Library and Information Professionals, *UK Survey of Library and Learning Resource Provision in Further Education Colleges 2003*, CILIP, 2003.

Corrall, S., *Strategic Management of Information Services: a planning handbook*, Aslib/IMI, 2000.

Council for Learning Resources in Colleges, *CoLRiC Guidelines for Self-assessment of College Learning Resource Services*, CoLRiC, 2002.

Dadzie, S., *Equality Assurance: self-assessment for equal opportunities in further education*, Further Education Development Agency, 1998.

Department of Education and Employment, *Structural Requirements and Health and Safety: circular no.10/96*, DfEE, 1996.

Department of Education and Science, *Area Guidelines for Sixth Form, Tertiary and NAFE Colleges: design note 33*, DES, 1983.

Department for Education and Skills, *Key Design Guidance for Schools*, DfES, 2003.

Further Education Funding Council, *Accommodation Strategies: guidance for colleges: supplement to circular 97/19*, FEFC, 1997.

Further Education Funding Council, *Guidance on Floorspace Management in Further Education Colleges: supplement to circular 97/37*, FEFC, 1997.

Further Education Funding Council, *Networking Lifelong Learning: an ILT development strategy for FE*, FEFC, 1999.

Hannagan, T., *Management: concepts and practices*, Financial Times Management, 1998.

Jenkins, C. and Morley, M. (eds), *Collection Management in Academic Libraries*, Gower, 1999.

Joint Funding Councils' Libraries Review Group, *Report: a report for the HEFCE, SHEFC, HEFCW and DENI (The Follett Report)*, HEFCE, 1993.

Kerr, G., Get to Know Your Stock, *Library Association Record*, **100** (2), February 1998, 78–81.

Lee, S. and Boyle, F., *Building an Electronic Resource Collection: a practical guide*, 2nd edn, Facet Publishing, 2004.

Library and Information Statistics Unit, *Library and Statistics Tables*, LISU, 2002.

McDonald, A., *Moving Your Learning Resource Service*, Aslib, 1994.

McDonald, A., *Space Requirements for Academic Libraries and Learning Resource Centres*, SCONUL, 1996.

Mitchell, D. J. (ed.), *Belfast '96 Designs on Learning: proceedings of the CoFHE annual study conference held at Stranmillis College, Belfast, 1st-4th April 1996*, CoFHE, 1997.

Mitchell, D. J. (ed.), *Library Design: principles and practice for the college librarian*, CoFHE, 1992.

OFSTED, *Handbook for Inspecting Colleges*, OFSTED, 2001.

Resource, *Better Public Libraries*, Resource (now MLA), 2003.

Rogers, L., New British Libraries: sector report learning resource centres, *Royal Institute of British Architects: Interiors*, October 1995.

Scottish Further Education Funding Council, *Resources and Services Supporting Learning: a service development quality toolkit*, SEFC, 2003.

Society of College, National and University Libraries, *The Quality Assurance Agency for Higher Education – Aide-mémoire for Reviewers Evaluating Learning Resources*, SCONUL, 2003.

Society of College, National and University Libraries, *The SCONUL Vision*, SCONUL, 2003.

University for Industry, *Design for Learning*, UfI, 2003.

Index

Please note that the numbers refer to sections, *not* pages.

The Academic Library
Second edition

PETER BROPHY

Reviews of the previous edition
'*The Academic Library* should be on every student librarian's core reading list.'
INFORMATION WORLD REVIEW

'An excellent book...Peter Brophy has achieved a worthy and useful summary of the academic library at the start of the new millennium.'   SCONUL NEWSLETTER

This authoritative and wide-ranging textbook provides a comprehensive overview of the changing functions of higher education libraries and the organizational cultures in which they operate. It offers an assessment of the impact of such changes on service delivery from both provider and user perspectives, and considers the future role of the academic library.

The second edition has been completely updated, with a new chapter on performance measurement and more extensive coverage of: accessibility; information literacy; portals; digital libraries; copyright; institutional repositories; virtual and managed learning environments; and management of change. Written in a readable and accessible style, the book focuses on:

• the library in the institution
• users of the academic library
• the impacts and opportunities of ICTs
• human resources
• management and organization of resources
• collection and access management
• the academic library building
• library systems and networks
• specialist services
• management and professional issues
• the academic library of the future.

This textbook is an indispensable introduction to the range of issues facing academic libraries for students and new professionals. It also makes stimulating reading for education administrators and academic library managers in both higher and further education.

2005; 248pp; paperback; 1-85604-527-7; £32.95

Supporting e-learning
A guide for library and information managers

Edited by MAXINE MELLING

E-learning is becoming commonplace in academic institutions. To date it has been used as an alternative medium in the delivery of established content; however, it is also becoming a vehicle for much wider ranging developments, including a change in the relationship between teachers and those responsible for learner support. Increasingly library and information services are directly involved in the development of e-content and in delivering services to support e-learning. Thus it is affecting all aspects of library service provision in education.

This management guide takes a practical and strategic approach to providing quality services in an e-learning environment. It will help managers understand e-learning and, more importantly, help them exploit the full potential of this new area for their service. Contributions from leading managers and practitioners address the range of operational issues that managers should consider in supporting e-learning, and provide case studies in order to demonstrate how the theory can be translated into practice. Key areas covered include:

- managed learning environments (MLEs)
- process and partnerships
- change management
- support in the use of new media
- e-literacy in the wider perspective
- collection management.

This book is essential reading for all managers of library and information services involved with policy and service development issues, from senior to team managers. It will also be insightful for new professionals and students.

The contributors
Stephen Clarke, Frances Hall, Robert Hunter, Jill Lambert, Oleg Liber, Frank Moretti, Sarah Porter, Michelle Shoebridge, Peter Stubley.

2005; 192pp; hardback; 1-85604-535-8; £39.95

Teaching Information Skills
Theory and practice

JO WEBB and CHRIS POWIS

Teaching information skills and using technology to empower users is now a crucial part of most information professionals' jobs, but very few have been formally trained to teach. In order to be effective at teaching and supporting learning it is necessary to take a professional approach and to understand the processes involved in learning. This practical book shows the reader how to implement vital teaching skills in their role as information manager.

The text covers both the theory and the practice of library instruction. Each chapter has two parts: a section explaining the principles of learning and teaching, followed by a section analysing successful learning and teaching activities, rooted in personal experience. The book draws best practice examples and case studies from a broad range of sectors and organizations. Each of the main chapters is based around one of the key elements of successful learning and teaching, specifically applied to the LIS context:

- learners and learning styles
- motivating learners
- auditing: finding out what your learners need
- planning a learning experience
- delivery: tools, techniques and approaches
- assessment
- feedback and evaluation
- building a teaching team.

All library and information professionals who have to instruct others – either students or colleagues – as part of their job, whether working in an education, public, health or workplace library context, need this book. It is an essential text for library school students as the subject becomes more widely taught.

2004; 240pp; hardback; 1-85604-513-7; £39.95